K. G. PONTING

Discovering

Textile History and Design

SHIRE PUBLICATIONS LTD

Contents

Preface

Textile history and design is a wide subject and such an introduction as this has to be selective. In the section of Chapter 3 devoted to woven design some technical detail has been given because it was felt that many people today interested in weaving will find it useful. This section can be omitted without affecting the chapter as a whole.

The author expresses his thanks to the many people who over the years have answered questions and helped in other ways to forward his interest in textiles and their history, above all the staff at the Victoria and Albert Museum, whose kindness and help can never be adequately repaid. It must be said, however, that the author alone is responsible for what is said in this volume.

All the photographs are reproduced by kind permission of the Victoria and Albert Museum (Crown Copyright). The design diagrams are by Richard G. Holmes.

Cover photograph: Detail of a Saracen killing a bear, from the Devonshire Tapestry. (Victoria and Albert Museum, Crown Copyright.)

Copyright © 1981 by K. G. Ponting. First published 1981; reprinted 1986. Number 261 in the Discovering series. ISBN 0 85263 551 6.

Set in 9 on 9 point English Times by Permanent Typesetting & Printing Co Ltd, Hong Kong, and printed in Great Britain by C. I. Thomas & Sons (Haverfordwest) Ltd, Press Buildings, Merlins Bridge, Haverfordwest.

1. Introduction

Textiles are all pervading; indeed, like architecture they are almost impossible to avoid. One might go through life without looking at a painting, a drawing or a piece of sculpture, but it would be difficult not to see a building or look at a piece of fabric. Indeed, one suspects that the attraction of a good cloth design on a pretty girl has given more people pleasure than even the finest of paintings. This is not to argue that textile art rates as high as painting and sculpture, but the division that has become common in western countries, into major and minor groups of arts, did not apply in the east. In China and India the potter and the weaver occupied a place equal to that of the painter or sculptor. It is impossible to deny the highest possible place to such textiles as the medieval tapestries at Angers, the Wavel tapestries at Cracow, the Hunting tapestries at the Victoria and Albert Museum, the fine Turkish carpets, also at the Victoria and Albert Museum and at Vienna, the Turkish tents at Cracow, the Syon Cope and many other examples of English medieval embroidery. There are many sections of textile design; woven is the most common and usually means a combination of weave and colour to give the overall effect. Printed designs are normally produced on a plain woven fabric made in plain weave by one of the three main methods of direct printing, namely hand, roller or screen. Usually included among printed textiles is a rather different group which is better described as pattern-dyed. These include the beautiful Batik designs from Java and the tie and dye effects from many centres.

Carpets are special forms of woven fabric. The best ones made by machines are the so-called pile carpets, in which certain of the ends, after being inserted in the cloth, are cut so that what one sees is not so much the yarn as the pile composed of individual fibres standing upright. It is easy to see the difference in design this necessitates. Pile carpets derive from the traditional knotted carpets which have been made for centuries. With these the carpet weaver knotted his pile on to a plain weave background which lay out of sight.

Tapestry weaving is completely different. The weft does not go right across the piece but is inserted to whatever width is required to produce a figure or pattern. Many people consider tapestry the most artistic form of textile, but it can be argued that too often the tapestry weaver has attempted to copy in a textile design what the painter does better. Perhaps the mediocre pieces often seen have led to this feeling; the finest examples, such as those already mentioned at Angers, Cracow and in London show clearly what can be done.

3

Embroidery is sometimes confused with tapestry, the most obvious case being the famous Bayeux tapestry, which is a fine piece of embroidery. With tapestry the pattern is made in the actual weaving, whereas with embroidery plain fabric is taken and the pattern threaded in afterwards. In the past embroidery has perhaps been the type of design in which the highest degree of artistic skill has been lavished. The great treasures of English medieval embroidery, so well represented at the Victoria and Albert Museum, show textile design at its finest level. The individual artist has freedom to develop his ideas and the great traditions of Opus Anglicanum, literally 'English work' but meaning embroidery, beginning with Saxon pieces such as St Cuthbert's stole and continuing throughout the middle ages, is one of Britain's greatest contributions to art.

Lace represents another technique, unconnected with weaving. Design in lace lies in the structure of the fabric in a different way to any other type of fabric so far described. From the seventeenth century lace was regarded as one of the greatest of textile arts, and although in the twentieth century it has been less favoured a return to popularity may well be coming. Fine pieces of lace can still be obtained at reasonable prices.

Lace has an obvious link with knitting, now regarded as the main alternative method to weaving when making a fabric. Recently knitting has captured a large part of the long established field of the traditional woven fabrics but historically knitted fabrics and particularly knitted designs have not presented quite the fascination of the other forms. It was mainly knitted plain and most great styles of the past have involved fancy work. There were, however, exceptions – fine ecclesiastical knitted gloves exist – and in certain cases the craft knitter apparently had to knit a masterpiece before being admitted as a master knitter in his guild. Some areas such as the Shetland Islands developed distinctive designs, but they are not very numerous.

Two other types of fabric complete this introduction; neither have contributed as much to the overall picture of textile history and design as those given above. Of these two, felts, which involve neither spinning nor weaving, are fabrics made by exploiting the natural property of wool to felt. Although used in the west, these cloths have never rivalled woven fabrics. Their great area of production has been that vast country that lies south of the Caucasus and further east in Asiatic Russia. There design has played a part, but most felts are utilitarian rather than decorative. Secondly, there are several types of woven fabric best described as braids, which have been made in various ways over the ages, particularly in peasant cultures. They have been made in a great variety of design but have not produced great textiles like those represented in the other groups.

2. The history of textiles

The industrial crafts of spinning and weaving first appear with the neolithic or old stone age cultures of about 10,000 BC. Both must have been developed over long periods, with weaving perhaps coming first. It is possible to make a fabric out of long vegetable fibres without any spinning, and basketing, a very old craft, is basically the same as weaving. With the coming of well established neolithic cultures in the Nile valley, Mesopotamia, Crete and in the Indus valley and China, spinning and weaving were quickly developed.

From the dawn of history until the twentieth century man depended for the raw material of his textiles on four main natural fibres. Two, wool and silk, came from the animal world; two, cotton and flax, from plants. All are well represented in early archaeological remains and each of the four main early civilisations appears to have had a preference for one and particularly developed its use. The Egyptians used flax widely, the Sumerians wool; cotton appears to have been developed in the Indus valley and the Chinese long had a monopoly of silk.

For the western world flax and wool were the most important. Cotton was not known in the west during prehistoric times but was used in India by 3000 BC, when the civilisation of the Indus valley was at its height. Even during the following centuries this fibre never became widely known in the Mediterranean area, which is surprising considering that the Nile valley was to become one of the main cotton producing areas. Silk, perhaps the loveliest of all fibres, was one of the great natural products of the early Chinese civilisation and around 500 BC China was producing the best fabrics then made. As far as we can tell, the silk fabrics made in China at that time far surpassed in their technique and in their magnificence anything produced elsewhere.

The widespread nature of spinning in these early civilisations is clearly shown by the number of remains in the museums of the world. They are mainly of two types, spindles and whorls; there are more of the latter but the former were more important, as a brief history of early spinning will indicate. As spindles are easily mistaken for needles or small pieces of bone, many escape notice. Whorls were usually made of clay, the most indestructible material known at the time, hence their numbers. Spindles could also be made of wood and in this case were soon destroyed.

Originally, however, spinning would have been done entirely by the fingers without either spindle or whorl but production would have been extremely slow. To understand the development that followed, the main actions performed in spinning should be appreciated. First there is the drawing out of the fibre to form the yarn, a process now known as drafting, then the insertion of the twist to give the yarn sufficient strength, and finally the winding on of the thread to a convenient container.

The spinner drew out the fibre from the prepared mass of fibres by drafting between the two hands and inserting the twist as required. At some period it was recognised that a container for the yarn already spun was needed and this led to the use of a stick or similar tool for the purpose. Here was the first idea of a spindle, crucial in the development of spinning and perhaps the first great invention in the history of textile technology. It is impossible to overestimate the importance of the spindle in the development of the process.

Other geniuses realised that the spindle could be used in other ways to improve spinning. First, if it was tapered at one end and a notch was made on this tapered top, then the spinner could fasten the yarn already spun and use the spindle as a tool for transferring twist to the yarn being spun; to increase its effectiveness for this purpose a weighted whorl was placed at the bottom of the spindle.

The spindle is the longest lived tool in textile history, perhaps in all industrial history, because, invented by about 5000 BC, it is still basic in almost all forms of spinning. It combines three important technical uses, for it stored the yarn already spun, it inserted twist better than the fingers – anybody who doubts this could profitably try hand spinning and twisting by the fingers and compare it with using the spindle for this purpose – and it could be used for the drafting. The last use was probably not general because drafting between one hand and a falling spindle would have been less controllable than that between the two hands and only satisfactory with long and strong fibres. As spinning has developed, the spindle has remained important but is usually only used for the first two purposes, that is containing the yarn and inserting the twist.

Later another and larger stick called a distaff was added to the spinner's equipment and it carried the prepared fibre from which the material to be spun was taken, but a distaff is not essential for spinning, being merely a convenient means of carrying the material waiting to be spun.

With this fully developed spindle the hand spinner had an amazingly efficient instrument, as all who have seen a trained hand spinner working will agree. She continued to draw the fibre from the prepared mass by hand and could either do the drafting and the insertion of the small amount of twist needed to help the drafting with the other hand or could, if the material permitted, let the spindle fall to the ground, twisting it round and allowing the weight of it as it fell to draft the fibres at the same time, also letting twist pass through her fingers to make the whole process easier. When the drafting was completed, additional twist was needed to make the yarn strong enough for weaving and this came from the spindle now revolving on the ground. If the spindle was not used for drafting it could always be 'spun' on the ground and in this case any twist needed for assisting the drafting being done by the hands could be obtained by allowing it to slip through the fingers. It is probable that this would have been the most commonly used method and the use of the spindle as a drafting tool was likely to have been somewhat limited; but hand spinners could do either spindle drafting with twist or finger drafting only; simple hand spinning was in this way more adaptable than any machine has ever been.

Weaving may have predated spinning. Primitive people probably interlaced long vegetable stems (essentially basketwork) before they had acquired the skill necessary to convert short fibres into continuous yarns.

The earliest looms of which we have any information come from the Egyptians and it would appear that they had two types, the horizontal (with the yarn comprising the lengthwise part of the piece lying parallel with the ground) and the vertical loom, in which the warp hung at right angles to the ground. In early forms of weaving the crossing threads (the wefts) were interlaced by hand but very soon an arrangement was invented for dividing the warp threads so as to avoid this laborious hand work. The continuing slow improvement of this process has been the basis of the development of weaving.

Quite early on, the weft was wound on to a stick, thereby producing a primitive form of shuttle, and this made the interlacing between the warp threads much easier.

It seems that the commonest type of loom used in early civilisations was the vertical, normally in its warp-weighted form. One point of terminology emphasises this. Even today we still use the phrase 'beating up' the newly inserted weft pick to the fell of the cloth; this is really nonsensical in the horizontal loom. It is only in the vertical loom that one actually beats up the weft.

Both spinning and weaving occupied a great deal of time in early societies, the former especially as production was so slow. There are many references to them in classical literature.

There were exceptions to the almost universal use of spinning and weaving in early textile manufacture. Some very strong and long vegetable fibres could be used for making small pieces of fabric without spinning but the most important exception was with silk, where the silkworm had already produced continuous fibre so there was no spinning in the normal sense of combining short fibres to make a thread. The last two parts of the process of spinning, the twisting and the winding, were all that were needed and, with a fibre as fine as silk, they called for great care and attention. Unfortunately we are not well informed of the development of the reeling and the throwing (as silk twisting came to be called) in China, but later in medieval Europe the mechanical inventions in this field were important.

Wool has one unique property, namely its capacity to felt and form a thick solid fabric without any spinning or weaving but it is not known when this property was first utilised. Modern primitive races have made much use of bark fabrics and skins were widely used. There has long been an alternative method of making a fabric from yarn, today best exemplified by knitting, but this technique in its modern use of a continuous supply of yarn is comparatively recent and does not appear before about AD 1300. Other methods were known of making a fabric from a single thread as opposed to the weaving technique, which involved the crossing of two threads. Netting is the most obvious example, but 'sprang', which utilised a frame and existed in several distinct forms, is another technique with a long history.

Two other groups of processes which became important later had their beginning in primitive societies, those that prepared the fibres for the spinning and those which finished the fabric. Preparation methods depended on the type of impurity that had to be removed from the raw fibres. With wool it was the natural fat and the dirt that the sheep had collected, with cotton the seed, with flax the other vegetable matter, removed by a process known as retting, and with silk the gum which the silkworm had secreted. These operations were carried out in the simplest possible manner and, except in the case of cotton, consisted usually of treating the fibre with water and loosening or dissolving the impurities. With cotton the seed had to be laboriously picked out by hand. When the fibres were clean all entanglements had to be removed before spinning could be done. Combing, and later the alternative process of carding, separated the fibres. It was particularly necessary with wool but was done with all other fibres except silk.

The purpose of finishing is to convert the rather unattractive fabric coming from the loom into something which would appeal to the wearer. This did not apply to many early textiles, which were often worn in the condition in which they came from the loom. Most of the textiles we see in museums were made for special purposes, either for the decoration of the houses of kings and aristocrats or for their apparel. We have comparatively few remains of the textiles used by the poor.

Probably the finishing process was first developed on wool cloths. When washed, wool shrinks and the cloth is thereby thickened. By the Roman period fulling (deliberate shrinking) and the allied process of using teasels to obtain a skinlike finish on the cloth were well recognised processes.

Textiles have always depended for much of their attraction on their colour and dyeing had, by the period of the Roman empire, become one of the most important of all processes. The Romans produced excellent colours. Their most famous dye was woad, which is closely allied to indigo, the actual colouring matter in both being the same although it occurs in a more concentrated form in indigo. Indigo itself was hardly known in the west during early times but was widely used in India and the Far East. Woad was the common blue in the west, used both for colouring fabrics and colouring the skin, as described by Julius Caesar when he visited Britain.

The early dyer was well equipped with reds and two of these, madder and kermes, were among the most famous dyes of antiquity and gave colours of good fastness. Madder came from the root of the plant of the same name whereas kermes came from an insect which inhabited the oak trees of the eastern Mediterranean. The main source of the other primary colour, yellow, was a plant known as weld. With these dyes the ancient dyer could produce any shade required. There was no natural green which gave a permanent colour. When one considers how much green colour there is in nature, this is surprising. Greens were obtained by first dyeing with a yellow colouring matter such as weld and then over-dyeing with woad or indigo. It is because woad or indigo is a faster dye than weld that in some old tapestries the grass has turned to almost a blue.

In the Roman world Tyrean purple was the most expensive and famous of dyes. It became the symbol of high status in imperial Rome; to wear a purple gown was the prerogative of the wealthy and, later, in the Eastern or Byzantine empire this colour was reserved for members of the imperial family. It was obtained from a shellfish and as vast quantities of this mollusc were needed to obtain sufficient dye it was very expensive.

All these dyes were difficult to apply. Indigo, woad and Tyrean purple, which was closely allied chemically to the other two, were what are now known as vat dyes, which means that they were not soluble in water in the form in which they were obtained and they had to be reduced by a fermentation process. The material to be dyed was then dipped in the dye liquor and only took its permanent shade after the colour had been allowed to oxidise in the air; the depth of the shade obtained depended on the number of dips given. Madder and kermes, on the other hand, were mordant dyes and only permanently coloured the material when it had already been treated with another chemical. The ancient dyers did not know anything about the chemistry of the process and only acquired their knowledge of how to dye by trial and error. As a group of men they tended to be despised because, it was said, their hands were always dirty and, particularly in Rome, they smelt of fish. This was unfair; they were skilled craftsmen at least the equal of the weavers of the time.

Although there were many improvements, the basic technical methods outlined above continued to be used throughout most of the world until about AD 1000. There then occurred the most remarkable of all textile revolutions, one that in the range of its new discoveries far surpassed the much better known industrial revolution of the late eighteenth century.

There were four important new discoveries. In the spinning the simple spindle method was replaced by the wheel. In the preparation of the wool for spinning carding was introduced and to a considerable extent replaced combing. In the weaving the almost universal use of the upright loom was replaced by the horizontal loom, both in its narrow form and, probably more important, as a broad loom. Finally, in the finishing the ancient method of thickening woollen cloth by treading on it was replaced by fulling, using wooden hammers controlled by a waterwheel.

The last of these inventions has been the most widely discussed, largely because of the notable work done on this subject by Professor Carus-Wilson. In addition, it represents the first application of mechnical power to a textile process. It was, however, not as important as the coming of the spinning wheel. Fulling could only be applied to woollen cloth and, although woollen cloth was the most widely used type in the western world, it was not so popular in the other civilisations, notably those of China and India.

The coming of the spinning wheel was the outstanding new technique. The original home of the spinning wheel has not yet been ascertained. Indeed, it may have been invented more than once. It is not disputed that the spinning wheel was a Far Eastern invention, but it has not been decided whether it came first from China or India. It arrived in the west in about 1100 and was widely adopted in areas where there was a commercial textile trade. Where women were spinning merely for their own domestic use, they preferred to continue to use the simple spindle as they could carry it with them into the fields while watching the flocks.

The spinning wheel increased production about tenfold. This early spinning wheel was not the type of spinning wheel that is used today for craft spinning. It was much simpler, consisting merely of a wheel for driving a spindle, a simple mechanical version of the earlier hand idea. The spinning wheel normally used today has an apparatus called a flyer attached to it which enables twisting and winding on to be done together. This was invented in Europe around 1400 and did not replace the simple wheel just described. The wheel with the flyer was excellently adapted for spinning flax but was not so good with other fibres. It is sometimes called the Saxony wheel because it was probably invented in that part of Germany, which was famous for its production of flax.

Carding was a means of disentangling fibres before spinning by working them between two boards on to which pieces of leather, with wire teeth attached, had been placed. In this way the entanglements in the raw material could be easily removed and a rolag (or small roll of fibre) obtained which was ideally suitable for spinning on the wheel. Previously the entanglements in the raw material had been removed either with the fingers or by combing. Combing continued to be used, notably with flax, in which case it was called hackling. Carding was particularly suitable for wool but could also be used for cotton, although there is evidence to suggest that the entanglements in cotton, particularly in its native India, were more often removed by beating or bowing the fibre. This beating or bowing is remarkably effective but because it was never widely used in the west its importance has been underestimated.

As the silkworm provided a continuous filament of silk this only had to be twisted to make a yarn. Much of the silk, however, was damaged when being reeled from the cocoon and this could be spun on the simple spindle or the spinning wheel. There was also a species of silk known as wild silk which was processed in this way.

The horizontal loom made it easier to divide the warp threads to form more complicated patterns but in the west, where this loom was developed, it was mainly used for producing cloth woven in simple weaves which depended for their consumer appeal on the colour that was applied and the manner in which clothworkers produced soft handling effects on woollen cloth. The most interesting developments in the technique of weaving came from the east. The horizontal loom appeared early in China and there is some doubt whether the vertical loom ever had the popularity there that it did in the west. The Chinese, as early as 200 BC, had developed a loom which could weave complicated patterns. It is not certain how this loom worked but we do know that developments from it led, during the following centuries, to the introduction of the draw loom, which had a complicated but excellent system of dividing the warp threads so as to make patterns of almost unbelievable complexity. The comparatively few warp threads that worked the same were tied up to held cords; these were pulled in a predetermined manner by draw boys so that the weaver could insert his weft in the right order. The draw loom and the spinning wheel were the greatest inventions in the medieval history of textiles.

The mechanisation of fulling has been much more thoroughly written about than the other processes. Its importance was mainly confined to the western world, where it led to the removal of the woollen trade from the cities to the countryside, where water-mills, used for the grinding of corn, had already been established. It was probably the advent of the fulling mill that led to the development of the great European woollen textile trade of the later medieval centuries.

These four inventions established a routine in the manufacture of textiles that was to last from 1250 to 1750. There were new developments during this period, including the Saxony spinning wheel, but that was mainly used for flax. The two most interesting inventions were the silk throwing mill and William Lee's knitting frame, both in industries that lay outside the mainstream of spinning and weaving. The silk throwing machine was, after the draw loom, the most complicated apparatus invented to process textile materials in medieval times. Like the draw loom it was developed in China but, unlike the draw loom, it was adapted to be driven by water power, although it is not certain whether this adaptation took place in China. Silk throwing mills appeared in Italy, notably in Lucca, around 1300 and spread widely throughout Italy during the next two hundred years. The idea was brought to England by the brothers Lombe and they established what could be called the first British factory on the Derwent at Derby; this was one of the first recorded cases of industrial espionage. The knitting frame of William Lee was an almost equally ingenious invention. It increased production by something like ten times, comparable with the coming of the spinning wheel, but it did not have the same impact. During the two to three centuries following Lee's invention most knitting continued to be done by hand.

This system of textile manufacture lasted until about 1750. Several difficulties had long been apparent, among them the fact that the late medieval hand loom was a relatively efficient instrument which needed a large number of hand spinners to keep it going. The first of the inventions of the classic industrial revolution, namely Kay's invention of the flying shuttle, which made weaving much easier and virtually doubled production, consumed yarn even faster. For some years attention had been given to methods of increasing spinning production and in 1760 James Hargreaves, a Lancashire weaver, invented his jenny, which was really a kind of multiple spinning wheel. It was widely adopted and did not cause any labour problems, perhaps because it was, in its original form, turned by hand and so could be used by domestic workers. The only people who suffered were the women in outlying villages who had long depended on hand spinning to balance their family budget.

Almost contemporary with Hargreaves, Richard Arkwright produced a workable adaptation of an idea of Lewis Paul that the drafting of fibres which had previously been done between the fingers of the two hands, or between the fingers of one hand and the spindle of the spinning wheel, could be done by passing the prepared fibre – or rolags – between two pairs of rollers, of which the second pair revolved faster than the first. Although the idea was simple, the practical application was extremely difficult. It is to the great credit of Arkwright that he produced a frame that worked. However, the real success with machine spinning came with Samuel Crompton, who combined the two ideas previously developed by Arkwright and Hargreaves in his spinning mule, so called because it incorporated these two quite different principles. The industrial revolution of around 1800, which gave Britain the foremost place in the industrial world in the first half of the nineteenth century, depended essentially on the cotton trade and the industrialisation of cotton depended above all on Crompton's mule.

The mechanisation of weaving was a less exciting and slower process than that of spinning as there were no completely new ideas. The trade felt that power loom weaving was not possible and it was left for an eccentric but brilliant clergyman, Edmund Cartwright, to show that it was. Cartwright's loom was essentially a hand loom driven by power. A lot of work had to be done before it was satisfactory but by 1840 the power loom had taken over in the cotton trade and was about to take over in the wool trade in Britain. Other industrial nations followed quite quickly although in the more outlying areas, which were often those where flax was produced, hand looms continued to be used until the end of the century.

The finishing processes, too, were mechanised. The most important such change was the coming of roller printing. Perhaps the most interesting was the invention of the rotary shearing machine, which did away with the old method of shearing the surface of cloth with large hand shears and replaced it by the circular blade that is best known in the form of the lawn mower. Indeed, the lawn mower was an adaption of the invention made to shear cloth.

There was a later industrial revolution, the chemical revolution, by which the old natural dyes were, from 1865 onwards, replaced by chemical products. The processes of dyeing and printing, by which textiles are given their colour, began to be properly understood and, at the same time, the old method of patterning textiles, which had been done with wood blocks, was successfully mechanised at an earlier date by a Scotsman, Thomas Bell, who engraved the patterning on to rollers, thereby making the process continuous.

The chemical revolution, based on the introduction of synthetic dyes, led to an increasing dominance of chemistry in textile processing and this was to culminate in the twentieth century when chemists added to the fibres in common use by producing others in their laboratories. First came rayon, which had many of the properties of cotton, and then nylon, terylene and others, which had entirely new and in some ways competitive characteristics. These man-made or synthetic fibres have been of great value but they have not replaced the natural ones. Silk still remains the most lovely of fibres and wool perhaps the most comfortable to wear. Cotton is still the most widely used of all. Nor have the synthetic fibres yet produced the beautiful fabrics that have been made in the past from natural fibres.

In the twentieth century there has been a revival in what one might call craft textiles, namely the making of textiles by hand. It probably stemmed originally from William Morris and his revolt against machines. Many lovely fabrics are made in this way, some of them the most attractive produced today. Usually the craft worker prefers to work with the traditional fibres, particularly silk or wool, although increasing use is being made of the synthetics. The craft worker should be careful not to become too tied to the past, as has happened with dyeing in its various forms, including printing, for problems have arisen from the inflexible use of the old natural dyes when better and brighter effects could be produced with the synthetics. Some lovely modern fabrics have been produced by applying synthetic dyes by long established techniques.

With modern as with older textiles, it is important to see as many of the great examples as possible at the museums listed in chapter 5.

3. Types of fabric

Woven design: plain weave

With woven design it is necessary to differentiate between types which have traditionally been called plain and fancy. P[lain] designs are those that can be made in a simple loom, usually eit[her] the so-called plain weave, where each end and pick works exa[ctly] opposite to the next, or the common (2/2) twill. Although col[our] and weave effects are obtainable in the plain weave, more of[ten] these cloths are solid coloured and are either utilitarian or have a finish that is developed in the later processes.

Broadcloth is historically the great example of this type of cloth. The name was originally used to describe cloths that had been woven in the broad as opposed to the narrow loom. The broad loom, which was about 120 inches wide (3m), appeared in Europe around the thirteenth century. The weaver sat at the side of his loom and threw the shuttle across to his assistant (with the narrow loom he sat in front). This cloth was usually spun, woven and fulled in the white, then dyed in the piece and 'clothworked' with teasels to develop a fine nap, which was then cut down to an even surface, so giving a skinlike finish. Broadcloth varied from the fine (made of merino wool) to the coarser types and was used throughout Europe between 1250 and 1850. It was the main woollen cloth made at the time and was almost always made in the plain weave; the appeal lay in the colour and handle, not in the design or patterning.

Woven design usually means a combination of weave and colour effect. Printed design, although produced on a plain woven fabric, usually made in the plain weave, depends for effect on the printed pattern. From the designer's standpoint the two groups are quite distinct; few, if any, would design in both fields. The first calls for a combination of technical ability and artistic imagination, with the former predominating. The artistic problem of the designer of woven fabrics is to operate in a limited field where the technical problems are to the fore. With printed fabrics the problems are different and although technical knowledge is important it is secondary. Consequently workers in other branches of design, distinguished painters even, are often asked to provide designs for printed fabrics but it would be useless to ask them to do this for woven fabrics. For this reason most textile firms specialising in woven design employ design staff within their own organisation, whereas firms working with printed textiles often buy their designs from outside.

There are a number of weaves that give a distinctive effect without help from the colour. Perhaps the best known examples are the Bedford cord, which gives a rib running up and down the

15

fabric, and the Cavalry twill, which gives an attractive twill running across the fabric and has always been traditional for hunting dress.

In most cases, however, it is the combination of weave with colour that constitutes woven or cloth design. Fabrics made in this way have been and remain the most common type for apparel and consequently call for more detailed consideration. The plain weave, in which end and pick interlace exactly opposite each other, is excellent for solid-coloured cloths but less versatile for weave and colour effects. But much can be done: for example, if this plain weave is coloured one thread light and one thread dark, a neat hairline effect is produced.

The traditional way of writing out woven designs is to use squared paper and then insert crosses where the warp passes over the weft. Thus the plain weave can be represented as shown in design 1. A reasonable idea of how this weave would appear in the cloth if woven one light one dark can be given as in design 2.

Checks can be made by group colourings; the 4 light 4 dark can be taken as an example. Alternatively the hairline colouring shown above can be combined with another colouring such as the 2 and 2 to produce a check (see design 3).

Design 1

	X		X
X		X	
	X		X
X		X	

Design 2

		X		X
L		X		X
D	X		X	
L		X		X
D	X		X	
	L	D	L	D

Design 3

		x		x		x		x
D		x		x		x		x
D	x		x		x		x	
D		x		x		x		x
D	x		x		x		x	
L		x		x		x		x
L	x		x		x		x	
L		x		x		x		x
L	x		x		x		x	
	L	L	L	L	D	D	D	D

Perhaps the most interesting design developments made in the plain weave came in the nineteenth century and involved the use of twist or other fancy yarn. Twist yarns, where two or more yarns are twisted into one, have had a long history. They are usually yarns of the same colour and the object is to increase the strength: a yarn made of two threads twisted together will be much stronger than a single thread of the same thickness as the doubled one. The manufacture will, however, require much more work, as the spinning is twice as fine and then there is the doubling to do. Where the strength was vital, as for example with yarn for knitting stockings, there were laws and regulations demanding that the yarn used should be two-ply or even three-ply. The interest for a designer is in the colouring possibilities when two yarns of different colours are combined. This idea probably originated in the Lowlands of Scotland, where during the nineteenth century the colouring of simple weaves was developed to new degrees of subtlety. Such cloths were known under a variety of names, thornproof for example, stressing that this plain weave, especially when made from twist yarn, is very hard wearing and not easily damaged.

There are many other types of fancy yarns with loops or slubs, which give interesting effects in the plain weave. Perhaps the best known is the Donegal tweed, made from woollen yarns which, during carding, have been covered with brightly coloured flecks or slubs. These cloths were originally produced, and are still made, in County Donegal but the name, like so many others, is now used more generally.

The plain weave can be developed in several ways. Two are important, the matt and the cord or rib. The matt or hopsack weave can be of any size although there is a practical limit. The 2/2 hopsack is very useful and interesting (design 4). Most colouring effects are as for the plain weave with each unit multiplied by two, but there is an important exception: when coloured 1 and 1, in practice usually combined with a 2 and 2 colouring, a distinctive check effect is obtained but it does have weaving problems. The first and second ends must be split in the reed or they will cross over in weaving and a nasty fault will occur in the cloth. This involves a very fine reed causing special weaving problems such as the difficulty of getting the knots to go through. In addition it is difficult to avoid the same trouble occurring in the weft.

		X	X			X	X
		X	X			X	X
X	X			X	X		
X	X			X	X		
		X	X			X	X
		X	X			X	X
X	X			X	X		
X	X			X	X		

Design 4

Cord or rib weaves are historically even more interesting. They can be made either as weft (design 5) or warp (design 6) cords and in a warp cord the warp tends to show on the surface and with a weft cord, the weft does; the latter is more often used and can be developed into an interesting form of figure weaving. If one looks at the warp cord weave it will be noticed that the warp interlaces 2

17

and 2 with the weft, whereas the weft interlaces 1 and 1 with the warp and the effect of this is for the weft to lie straight in the centre of the cloth with the warp showing on the face and the back. The warp cord is therefore excellent for stripes and in mechanical weaving this is probably the most used of these weaves. The weft cord has the opposite qualities and if a hand weaver wishes to weave tapestry-like effects in the simplest possible way then this weave is an excellent basis.

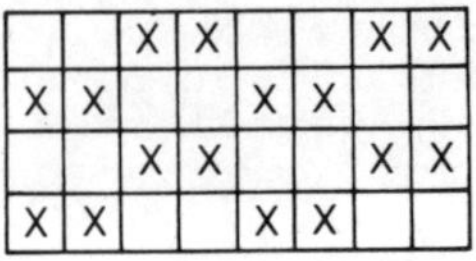

Design 5

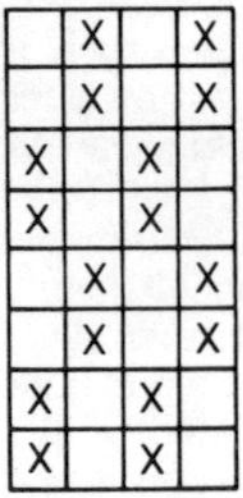

Design 6

The 2/2 or common twill is as important historically as the plain weave. It was used almost as early and, once developed, had certain advantages, most notably in its ease of weaving. Many of the cloths on the upright loom, which was so widely used, were 2/2 twill and, even after the introduction of the broad loom had brought the plain weave dressed cloth to the fore, twills woven on either the upright, or increasingly on the narrow, horizontal loom, became important. The well known kersey and later the serge were both made in this weave. It is the ideal weave for the modern craft weaver to use and develop. The most usual way of using the 2/2 twill is by colouring with different colours in the warp and weft.

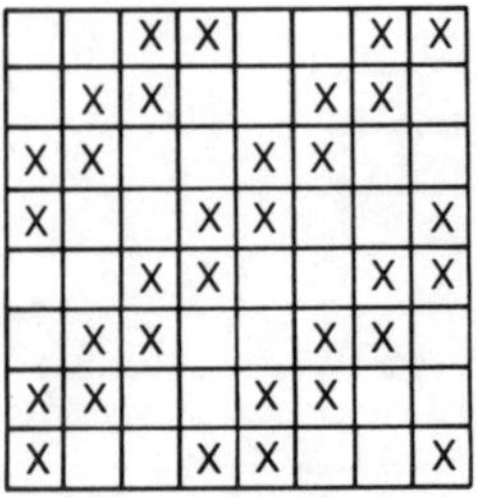

Design 7

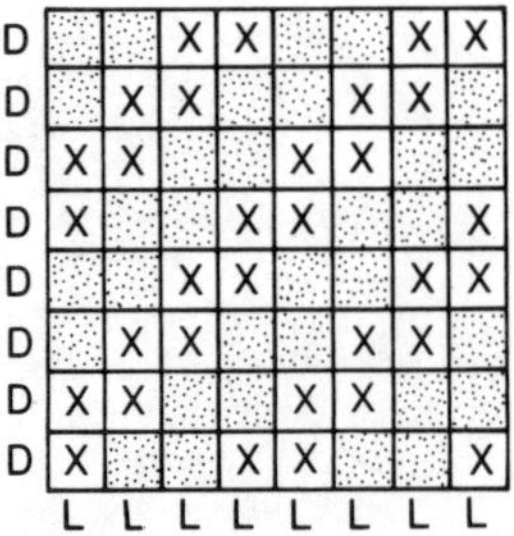

Design 8

Even better than using the twill weave straight is reversing it to form the well known herringbone shown in design 9. This change is obtained by simply altering the drafting and there is no need to alter the tie-up of the loom.

Design 9

		X	X			X	X
	X	X		X			X
X	X			X	X		
X			X		X	X	

Almost all colour combinations are possible in the 2/2 twill. The simple 1 and 1 colouring gives the very attractive pick and pick, a most attractive design, particularly if neatly coloured in relatively thick yarns. It is excellent for tweed effects and can be developed in several ways, for example to form herringbone and diamonds, but the straight effect is the more common and besides its use for ladies' cloths today it has often been made in fine worsted for men's wear. Indeed, a capacity to make a good pick and pick has always been a hallmark for the fine worsted cloth manufacturer. However, if the yarn should be uneven few cloths will show up bad effects so quickly.

Colouring the 2/2 twill two and two is equally popular and the result is the well known hairline. Variations are easily obtainable: the 2 and 2 combined with the 4 and 4 colouring gives the Glen check and the 2 and 2 can equally well be combined with the 1 and 1, but this colouring has never been so popular, probably because the check obtained is less well defined. Alternatively the warp colouring may be 2 and 2 and the weft solid. All the possible combinations of colourings are of outstanding importance. For example, in these 2 and 2 effects quite different appearances will be obtained if the two colours in the warp are different from those in the weft.

The 2/2 twill coloured 4 and 4 gives the well known Shepherd check (design 10), which is popular in all types of fabric and gives distinctive results, particularly if well coloured. It is possible to combine different colours in warp and weft but the results are probably not as good as with the 2 and 2. If one wishes to add further colourings to this combination it is better to do it in another way. For example, instead of all four colours being repeated, another additional third colour can be introduced. When this is done care must be taken that the basic colouring principle of using two colours distinct in tone is maintained, otherwise the distinctive effect of the Shepherd check will be lost. Other interesting variations can be obtained depending on how this design is woven and whether the difference is obtained by starting with the first pick of the design or the third. A hand loom weaver will find that many subtle variations can be obtained in this way.

Design 10

	L	L	L	L	D	D	D	D
D			X	X			X	X
D		X	X			X	X	
D	X	X				X	X	
D	X			X	X			X
L			X	X			X	X
L		X	X			X	X	
L	X	X				X	X	
L	X			X	X			X

Tartans should always be made in the 2/2 twill. Copies in the plain weave do not look right. Tartans were originally the mark of individual clans and the colour combination was intended to blend well with the Scottish scenery. This would not apply to the tartan designs commonly known today but there is evidence that many of these have little connection with the old traditional tartans, which are usually in more muted colours. The best known tartan today is perhaps the Black Watch, a good green, navy and black combination. The Royal Stuart is more colourful and there are many others listed in books that deal with tartan designs.

There are many other weaves suitable for plain as opposed to fancy designing. But the plain weave and the 2/2 twill will dominate the picture and if these comparatively simple cloths are not those one sees most frequently at textile museums this should not lead to their importance being misunderstood. If, for example, one looks at paintings it is likely that an eighteenth-century Englishman will be wearing broadcloth woven in the plain weave (the Scottish painter Ramsay painted broadcloths outstandingly well) and any nineteenth-century Scotsman will be wearing a tartan, made in the 2/2 weave and coloured in the traditional manner.

Woven design: fancy weave

Many of the more lovely and also most complicated fabrics were made in single cloth constructions, that is only one series of warp and one series of weft threads were used. The silks of the Han dynasty of China, many of the luxury Italian fabrics of the Renaissance and the textile silks from Lyons were made in this way. There are several possibilities but the most satisfactory is probably the method of designing, called damask, which consists of combining a warp-surfaced (design 11) and a weft-surfaced (design 12) weave to provide the shapes required. The basis can be, and often has been, the simple sateen.

	X	X	X	X		X	X	X	X
X	X		X	X	X	X		X	X
X	X	X	X		X	X	X	X	
X		X	X	X	X		X	X	X
X	X	X		X	X	X	X		X
	X	X	X	X		X	X	X	X
X	X		X	X	X	X		X	X
X	X	X	X		X	X	X	X	
X		X	X	X	X		X	X	X
X	X	X		X	X	X	X		X

Design 11

		X					X		
				X					X
	X					X			
			X					X	
X					X				
		X					X		
				X					X
	X					X			
			X					X	
X					X				

Design 12

Most of the patterning comes from the fact that the light reflection of the warp and weft surfaces will vary. Linen damask, almost always in white, depends entirely on this light effect for showing the weave. Colours can be introduced but if they are too contrasted spots of the warp will show in the weft sateen and spots of the weft on the warp part.

It was the difficulty of covering the other colour that led to the introduction of extra series of warp or weft for making fancy cloths. Figuring with extra weft was probably the first to be used; on the hand loom it is the simpler method and gives greater variety. The fancy colour is stitched to the back of the face cloth and then brought to the face when required. Theoretically, an almost infinite variety of patterning can be obtained in this way.

B	/	Ø	/	/	/	Ø	/	/	/	Ø	/	/				
F			X	X			X	X			X	X			X	X
B	Ø	/	/	/	Ø	/	/	/	Ø	/	/	/				
F		X	X			X	X			X	X			X	X	
B	/	/	/	Ø	/	/	/	Ø	/	/	/	Ø				
F	X	X			X	X			X	X			X	X		
B	/	/	Ø	/	/	/	Ø	/	/	/	Ø	/				
F	X			X	X			X	X			X	X			X
	F	F	F	F	F	F	F	F	F	F	F	F	F	F	F	F

F   Face
B   Back picks used for fancy work
X   Face weave
/   Face ends over fancy
Ø   Face under fancy for stitching

Design 13

Extra weft figuring has been popular with primitive peasant cloths, perhaps because bold effects can be easily obtained. More sophisticated civilisations have tended to prefer the single weave effects outlined previously.

Most of the great woven textile designs of the past have been made either by complicated single weave designs or by extra weft figuring. Since the introduction of power loom weaving there has been a change and extra warp figuring has replaced extra weft figuring. The main reason for this is the difficulty of inserting complicated wefting colour schemes in the power loom.

Extra warp figuring is technically very similar to extra weft figuring as the simple example (design 14) indicates.

X   Face weave
\   Back warp on face for figuring
●   Back warp stitched to back of face

Design 14

One very important method of obtaining fancy weaves remains to be considered, namely double cloth structures. They can be subdivided in several ways for example: (a) double plains – interchanging plain weaves; (b) cloth which has both warp and weft figuring, so for at least part of the fabric there is a double cloth structure; (c) self stitched double cloths; (d) extra stitched double cloths.

In (a) two plain weave cloths are woven together and held as one by being interchanged. The design produced tends to be angular and unsophisticated and can be easily recognised. Historically they are of interest because peasant communities with advanced weaving skills have often used them, notably in

Scandinavia, perhaps because, being double cloths, they are thick and therefore suitable for cold climates.

		X			\	X	\
\	V	\			V		
X				X	\		\
\		\	V				V
	\	X	\			X	
	V			\	V	\	
X	\			\	X		
			V	\		\	V

X   Face weave
V   Back weave
\   Lifting face ends over back picks
N.B. Each end and pick interchange from face to back every 4

Design 15

In (b) fabrics with warp and weft figuring are not very common as most of the effects obtainable can be achieved as well with extra warp or weft colouring.

Design 16

	F1	F2	F3	F4	F	B	F	B	F	B	F	B
B	/	⊘	/	/				V				X
F			X	X		\	X	\		\	V	\
B	⊘	/	/	/	V				X			
F		X	X		X	\		\	X	\		\
B	/	/	/	⊘			V					V
F	X	X				\	X	\		\	X	\
B	/	/	⊘	/	V				V			
F	X				X	\		\	X	\		\
4 F			X	X				X	•	X		
3 F		X	X				X	•	X			
2 F	X	X			X	•	X					
1 F	X			X	X					X		

X   Face weave
/   Face weave over back
⊘   Back weave stitched to face
\   Interchange of back to face
V   Interlacing of cloth at interchange
•   Stitching over face
N.B. Ends of 1-4 can be extended for any number

The other two types (c and d) are true double cloth structures. Two single fabrics are woven together and stitched into one, either (c) by occasionally arranging for the threads of one to interlace with the weft of the other, or vice versa (design 17), or (d) by using extra stitching threads (design 18). The advantage of the second method is that with the two cloths separate they can be made in more greatly contrasting colours. Double cloth structures of this nature are widely used today to obtain cloths with different colours on the face and back.

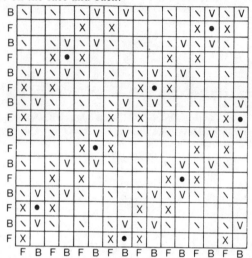

| X | Face weave | V | Back weave |
| \ | Face lifters over back | ● | Stitching together |

Design 17

Originally, fancy cloths were made by finger interlacing. On the upright loom the simple plain weave structure could be obtained by using two harnesses and the complicated figure patterning was added by hand. The warp-weighted loom, using a weft cord rather than the actual plain weave, would have been ideal, as anyone who has seen a warp-weighted loom being used will appreciate. At some period, probably in China, mechanised methods of operating the figure threads were invented and these led to the draw loom, one of the greatest of weaving tools. The fancy threads were worked by heddles tied together and operated by a draw boy, usually sitting above the loom. The draw loom increased the scope for figure weaving by making it unnecessary to have a series of plain ends and picks as before. All the ends and picks could play their part in the figured design.

Most of the great fancy cloths of China and, later, of Europe were made on the draw loom. The next invention was equally

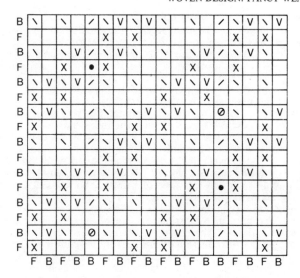

X   Face   V   Back
\   Face lifter on back
/   Stitching over back to bring to centre of cloth
•   Stitching over face
Ø   Stitching dropped under back weave

Design 18

remarkable. Jacquard, a weaver from Lyons, invented the loom, or correctly the mechanism that is attached to the loom, that still bears his name. It did away with the draw boy and replaced him by a punched card which indicated which heddles were to be up and which down. Jacquard's invention was the first of all memory-storing mechanisms. On it the most varied and extremely complicated designs can be made.

There are a number of special woven constructions, of which two are outstanding: velvets and gauzes. Velvets are woven in such a way that some of the warp ends or weft picks can be cut, thereby forming a pile. During the sixteenth century Italian velvets were the most luxurious and splendid of all cloths. Gauzes are light fabrics whose specific quality lies in the crossing of one set of warp threads upon another and the constant lifting of the same threads in every shed, the fabric being formed by the interposition of the weft between the crossed warp threads.

Printed and patterned dyed fabrics

These fabrics can be divided into those coloured by direct printing and those subjected to various types of resist printing which are in many ways nearer to dyeing and have had as long a history as true printing. Most of the great Indian prints, which arrived in Europe in the seventeenth century and caused a sensation, were made by a combination of both methods.

The main methods of direct printing are block printing, roller printing and screen and stencil printing. Block printing is the oldest and most traditional. During the industrial revolution a means was invented whereby the design, which had previously been cut on the block, could be cut on rollers and the whole process was greatly speeded without much loss of individuality. There has to be a separate block or roller for each colour and this is a limiting factor in this type of printing. Screen and stencil printing are newer inventions.

The importance in the history of textile design of roller printing techniques cannot be overestimated. One of the greatest changes in fashion and design that has ever occurred in Europe took place with the general introduction of calicoes (printed cottons). Cotton also became the fibre in commonest use. For example, in England at the beginning of the eighteenth century eighty per cent of fabrics made were from wool, the rest from flax or silk. By the beginning of the nineteenth century, eighty per cent were cotton, about sixteen per cent wool, the rest flax and silk. Cotton continued to be dominant and its position was only challenged in the twentieth century with the coming of the synthetics. Colour is applied to many of these by the roller printing technique originally developed for cotton.

Although printed cottons or calicoes were not known in the west before the great influx in the seventeenth century, straightforward printing on linen was an old European craft, probably introduced from the east during Roman times, when contacts between the east and the west were more numerous than they were to be again until the seventeenth century. Persia and Egypt were, perhaps, the direct sources rather than India, where the craft developed. Printing was practised in Europe in the fourth century and continued to flourish in Italy and Germany between the thirteenth and fifteenth centuries, but then it declined as the Renaissance introduced more luxurious ideas in cloth. The great textile revolution of the thirteenth and fourteenth centuries, particularly the development of the new loom, played a part in this change. Later, printing on linen enjoyed some revival in Europe, possibly after the lowering of living standards that resulted from the Thirty Years' War. These early printed linens, like their successors, the machine-printed calicoes of the eighteenth century, were usually worn by people of moderate means. For a time, when the gay colours of the first imported printed calicoes from India swept all before them, these fabrics were used by the more opulent classes and were seen by the wool manufacturers as a great threat to their prosperity, but with the coming of machines they tended once again to be used by the rising middle classes, while richer people turned to silk. The original Indian importations were often a combination of printed and resist work but the machine-made imitations that followed in nineteenth-century Europe were almost always entirely printed and were consequently much cheaper and less interesting in design.

However, the printing side of the Lancashire cotton trade was the most profitable during the great days. The first printing machine was built by Thomas Bell, a Scotsman, and was so fundamental an invention that its principles have been retained since, although numerous improvements and refinements have been added. Bell submitted a specification in 1783 and two years later commercial machine printing began at Mosney near Preston, Lancashire. Bell's machine was capable of doing the work of about forty hand printers and its effect on them was immediate, and without this invention it is difficult to see how the Lancashire cotton trade could have developed. There was an alternative type of printing machine, the Perrotine, in which the blocks were fixed in a moving part of the machine and then pressed on to the cloth. It was a clumsy method compared to roller printing and although it was widely used on the European mainland it was used very little in Britain.

Stencil and screen printing use a different technique. In stencilling the pattern is applied to the cloth by dabbing or spraying the colour round or through an independent plate or template. In screen printing a frame is used, over which is stretched a fine cloth screen. A resist, such as wax, is applied, in the shape of the design, to the screen, which is then lowered on to the material. The paint or dye, when applied, passes through the non-resisted parts of the fine cloth to the material below.

Tapestry

Tapestry is artistically the most important form of textile. The artist has almost completely free scope to build up the design as he wishes, much as a painter can use whatever colour he likes to put on his canvas. There is only one restriction, which will be dealt with later. Occasionally tapestry is confused with embroidery, the most notable example of this being the famous Bayeux tapestry, which is in fact an embroidery. With tapestry the fabric is built up as the design is made, whereas with embroidery one takes a plain fabric and embroiders the required pattern into the cloth.

Tapestry was made on an early development of the very simple version of the upright loom known to many early civilisations. Only a frame in which the warp ends can be tied between the top and the bottom is needed. The tapestry weaver can then interlace his weft yarns, which are the pattern-producing ones, as required. There is a well known painting on a Greek vase which shows this being done. One technical problem is important. As the weft, in addition to providing the pattern, has to hold the fabric together, there must be sufficient overlapping of one weft thread with another to obtain this. The most obvious fault in tapestry weaving is that this is not always done and sometimes old tapestries will be seen to have fallen apart where the colours join or to have been repaired by stitching.

Although the tapestry weaver can put in the colours as he requires, in the past it would seem that he did not always have complete artistic freedom. More often he was a craftsman producing a fabric from a cartoon, that is a painting made specifically to be copied by the tapestry weaver. The result is often a poor imitation of the painting. The Raphael cartoons in the Victoria and Albert Museum were made for this purpose. In the Raphael cartoon room at the museum the visitor can see a tapestry against the actual cartoon and there is little doubt which is the greater. However, a tapestry was not always a copy although even when the creator and the weaver were the same person it was usual for him to work from a sketch. This tendency of tapestries to look like imitations of paintings became more obvious after about 1600. Previously, as is so well exemplified in the works at Angers, one does not feel that one is looking at a copy. The Angers artist had sketches to work to, but the subordinate position of the craftsman to the creator, which is a fault in later works, had presumably not yet arisen.

Several different types of tapestry loom have been evolved, sometimes described as low and high looms, but all types are simple and entirely hand-operated. There has never been a mechanical tapestry loom.

Embroideries

There is some similarity between embroidery and printed design; one has to start with a plain fabric, usually plain woven, although it could be felt or, more likely today, knitted. Embroidery was one of the first methods used for adding fancy effects to plain knitted fabric, notably the so called clocks on knitted socks. But this was a specialised development and in general the basis for the great embroideries of the past was plain woven fabric and in many examples the plain fabric underneath is completely covered. Unlike tapestry, where the design is made as the fabric is produced and the necessary coloured wefts are added as required, in embroidery the colours that are required are sewn on to the fabric to produce the design. There is a common confusion between the two because the word 'tapestry' is wrongly applied to designs worked on canvas, originally in imitation of true tapestry, which are embroideries. England appears to have been the centre of the finest embroidery, whereas it was rarely the centre for the production of the greatest pieces of tapestry. To many who had come to regard embroidery as a poor relation of tapestry artistically the exhibition *Opus Anglicanum* organised by the Arts Council and the Victoria and Albert Museum was a revelation. No comparable display of English medieval embroidery had been assembled at any time since the Reformation. The great triumphs of Gothic art carried out in a medium such as this demonstrated the effects of colour in textiles. Those who missed the exhibition can still see many of the finest works in the Victoria and Albert Museum. They will not see the Pienza Cope, which was made in 1315 and is now in the cathedral at Pienza in Italy, but the famous Syon Cope, slightly earlier, is almost its equal, a superb example of the use of colour in textiles. Other masterpieces of this exhibition were the Cope of the Virgin from the cathedral of St Bertrand-de-Comminges in France and the Melk chasuble from Melk near Vienna. As for earlier work, the Bayeux Tapestry was probably made by English workers and shows the high quality of Anglo-Saxon embroidery. This is confirmed by the very fine stole of St Cuthbert, now at Durham. There must have been a long tradition behind the production of such works.

Carpets

The eminence given to tapestry, which is possibly challenged by embroidery, in the field of textile design could equally be challenged by carpets. The Persian carpets as exemplified by the masterpieces in the Victoria and Albert Museum rival the masterpieces of tapestry in all but range of design. The Persian carpet is only one form of the hand-knotted pile carpet which played an important part in eastern, particularly nomadic, life and the less ostentatious, simpler types of traditional peasant textiles are, in their own way, nearly as outstanding.

The pile carpet weaver has the same freedom as the embroiderer. He does not have to solve the major problem of the tapestry weaver of making both fabric and design at the same time. Each single knot is tied to the warp and the stability of the fabric is formed by putting a pick of weft right across the cloth. In other words, one has a fabric into which the pattern is knotted.

There is some doubt when knotted or pile carpets were first introduced. The recent discovery of the Pazyryk carpet suggests it was much earlier than previously thought. Carpets were certainly the basic craft of the Persians and the nomadic tribes of the area by the sixteenth century. The textiles so produced served many purposes and were not mainly used to cover the floor; they were more frequently wall coverings. The tents of the nomadic people were quite different from our conception of camping accommodation, becoming, in some cases, palatial in splendour, as exemplified by the tents of the Turkish emperor which were captured by the Polish king and are now in the museum at Cracow. Fine hand-made pile carpets continue to be made by the nomadic people of the area.

The carpet loom which the hand craftsman uses bears a close resemblance to the tapestry loom but, unlike tapestry weaving, carpet weaving was mechanised and the large quantities of carpets that are produced today bear little artistic relationship to the traditional carpets of the nomads.

The invention of a successful carpet-weaving loom taxed the ingenuity of western inventors. The problem was how to make the pile. The inventors had a base to work from because the making of a pile on a loom had been solved in the manufacture of velvets. One series of warp ends was cut with a knife, which was inserted almost as if it were a piece of weft and then withdrawn, cutting the warp, leaving a pile standing and showing on the surface. Compared with a hand-knotted carpet, production was much quicker but unless one was producing a carpet of one colour only, and this was not what the Persian or nomadic weaver was trying to do, the method was very wasteful in material because one had to have as many special warps as there were colours and when they were not wanted they had to be left in the middle of the carpet. Consequently Brussels carpets, the best known type, are so luxurious and today so dear that hardly anyone can afford to buy them.

Designers of carpet looms therefore set about finding some method by which loops of yarns resembling the knots of the carpet weaver could be embedded in the ground weave. They came up with a very ingenious idea. Small pieces of yarn were inserted into the cloth as it was being woven on a loom known as the Axminster, and for much of the late nineteenth century and early twentieth this loom produced most of the carpets for the western world. By the middle of the twentieth century a new technique was developed by which the loops were fixed in a gummy background, thereby obviating any weaving and producing the so called tufted carpets which dominate the bulk market today. None of these modern types of carpet has produced textiles of great artistic achievement, but as a means of adding comfort to the modern home there can be no doubt of their value.

Knitted fabrics

Several ways of making a fabric and of producing a design on it involve the intertwining of a single thread rather than the weaving of two series of threads, which has been the main basis of the sections already listed. Today by far the most important, in terms of production, of these single thread techniques is knitting.

The early history of knitting has not been satisfactorily worked out and to some extent the problem is one of definition. How does one define knitting? Probably the best way is as a fabric made by interlacing a continuous supply of yarn. This is not completely satisfactory and some add that the fabric must be made on needles. Taking the first definition, it would seem that knitting was originally invented somewhere in the Middle East and travelled, probably along the southern coast of the Mediterranean, to enter Moslem Spain, and it is from Spain that we have our first examples of true knitting.

It is, however, necessary to go back much earlier. Primitive people have since the neolithic period made fishing nets and perhaps from this tradition, notably in the northern countries where the warmth provided by any fabric made in this manner was so desirable, there evolved several techniques which have been described under a confusing number of titles, of which knotless netting is as good as any other. Such fabrics could be made in two ways: the yarns could be intertwined to form a fabric or the yarns could be intertwined with a kind of frame and then when the fabric was made the frames, or the rods of the frames, could be withdrawn leaving a fabric. In general terms this is a description of sprang and sprang appears very early in the history of textiles, long before true knitting.

There are other problems. For many years certain fabrics found in Coptic graves have been described as Coptic knitting but it has recently been shown that they are not knitting by the definition given above. Short lengths of yarn were interlaced to give an appearance like knitting. All these forms of fabric making produced essentially utilitarian objects but were not and were never intended as great art.

The position with true knitting is different because, when it appeared in European textiles, the first objects made were fancy work. This is shown by the remains preserved from the monastery of Huelgas near Burgos and the knitted gloves, mainly worn by ecclesiastics, which are found widely spread throughout western Europe. They are attractive but not great art and indeed, whenever knitting did attempt to achieve major artistic forms, it could be said to have failed. This is illustrated in some of the so called masterpieces that were made by knitting craftsmen under the guild system, particularly in Alsace and Silesia. These works, of which the best are in the museum at Colmar, are attractive but nobody would maintain that they are major works in the sense that tapestries of the same period are. It would appear that this was the feeling of most knitters and the great development of knitting, which began around 1500, was to be in the manufacture of plain fabrics, first of all for caps, which were heavily felted and whose attraction depended on their shape, and next in stockings. Suddenly, in Tudor England and in other European countries there was a desire for showing off one's legs, particularly by the male sex, and a knitted fabric does this better than a woven one. Stockings had been made from cloth cut on the cross but once knitting had arrived knitted socks soon took over. The brilliant invention by William Lee of his frame made the production of plain knitted fabric easier, and when decoration was wanted it was embroidered on. Consequently knitting, which has continued ever since to expand and has done much to make clothes warmer and more comfortable, cannot claim to occupy a very great space in the history of textile art. This applies even in the twentieth century, when knitted garments in their various forms comprise a larger section of the textile industry than those produced by weaving.

Lace

The most artistic form of non-woven textile is lace. Because the design in lace lies in the structure of the fabric rather than in any colour application, it could be argued that lace is the most fundamental of all textile arts. Hand-made lace came to the fore at the same time as knitting, although fulfilling a different purpose, being essentially a luxury article. There are two main types of hand lace: needlepoint and pillow. Both produce fine fabrics. There is also a form of machine lace, which has not achieved the artistic triumphs of the hand-made. The machine for making it was originally developed from the stocking knitting frame of William Lee, thus illustrating the basic similarity between the two processes, but later other and better methods were found.

Masterpieces of lace rank among the great achievements in textiles but are not quite the equal of the finest in embroidery, tapestry weaving and knotted carpets, perhaps because of the absence of colour. Nevertheless, because lace depends entirely on its structural effect, it has a distinctive place amongst textiles. Structure in textiles can be important and several attempts have been made, both in weaving and knitting, to achieve the same effect as lace. The honeycomb fabric in weaving and the Aran in knitting are examples.

Lacemaking came late to the textile scene but the well dressed man of the early seventeenth century, in addition to showing off his legs in knitted hose, used lace for decorative purposes. One

1. The Syon Cope is embroidered in coloured silks and silver gilt thread with the figures of Christ, the Virgin Mary and the Apostles. This detail shows Saint Thomas. English (Opus Anglicanum), early fourteenth century. (83-1864)

2. The Clare Chasuble; English, 1272-94. Silk embroidered with coloured silks and silver gilt and silver thread in split stitch, underside couching and laid and couched work. (673-1864)

3. Woman's jacket, English, c 1600. Silk embroidered with coloured silks and silver gilt and silver thread and spangled in sequins, with basket stitch and couched work. (173-1869)

4. *Franco-Burgundian tapestry depicting falconry. Second quarter of the fifteenth century. (T202-1957)*

5. Franco-Burgundian tapestry. Second quarter of the fifteenth century. Detail showing the quality of the original weave and restoration. (T202-1957)

6. *Tapestry depicting the War of Troy, woven in wool and silk at Tournai, last quarter of the fifteenth century. It derives from the famous set woven by Pasquier Grenier at the command of the magistrates of Bruges and presented to Charles the Bold, Duke of Burgundy. (6-1887)*

7. Flemish tapestry, 'The Three Fates'; early sixteenth century. Before restoration. (65-1866)

8. Sampler panel of English needlepoint lace; first half of the seventeenth century. Given to the Victoria and Albert Museum by Her Majesty the Queen. (T6-1910)

9. Italian needlepoint lace (Venetian); late sixteenth century.
(Hungerford Pollen Collection number 17)

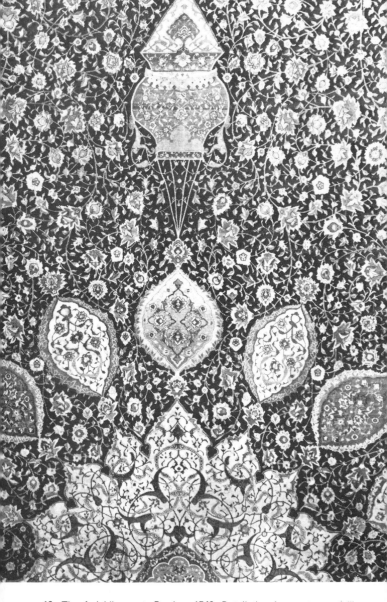

10. The Ardabil carpet; Persian, 1540. Detail showing centre medallion with lamp. (272-1893)

11. *Woven silk brocaded in colours on a damask ground; French, c 1740-50. (2028A-1899)*

12. *Cotton printed in red from engraved metal; French (Jouy; Oberkampf et Cie), late eighteenth century. (T371-1919)*

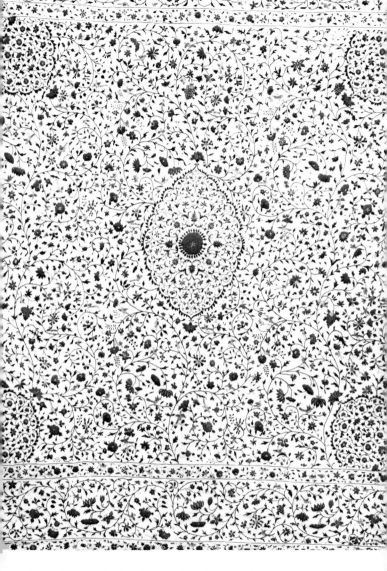

13. *Bedspread of painted cotton; East Indies, eighteenth century. (Circ 530-1923)*

14. Half woven coverlet — the Nine Snowball design; American, early nineteenth century. (T28-1923)

15. Double cloth; Peruvian (late Chimu). (T240-1932)

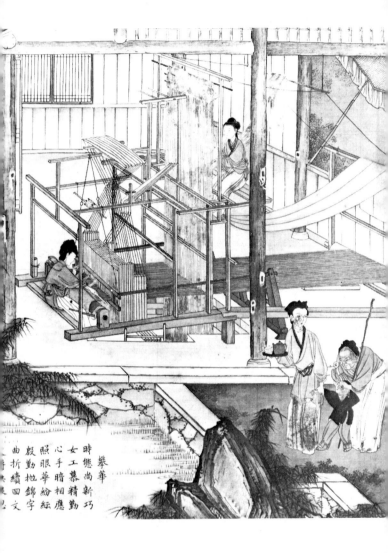

攀華

時應尚新巧
女工慕精勤
心手暗相應
照眼華紛綵
殷勤抛錦字
曲折續回文

16. *Original watercolour drawing depicting the weaving of figured satins, an illustration from 'Silk Culture and Manufacture', dating from the reign of the Emperor K'ang H'si (1662-1722). (D1656-1904)*

need only look at portraits of the Dutch school to appreciate how widespread this fashion had become.

The word lace is not easy to define. Lace is essentially ornamental openwork formed of threads of flax, cotton, gold or silver, which are looped or plaited or twisted together by hand, either using a needle, producing needlepoint lace, or with bobbins, pins and a pillow or cushion, in which case the work is known as pillow lace. Lacemaking, like tapestry, involves production of design and fabric concurrently. Pattern books for needlepoint and pillow lace date from about the middle of the sixteenth century. Before that period the word 'lace' described such articles as cords and narrow braids of plaited and twisted threads used not only to fasten shoes (the word 'shoelace' is still used), sleeves and corsets but also for decorative purposes – to braid the hair, wind around hats or to sew as trimming on costumes and quilts. The word is used in this sense by Leonardo da Vinci in the notes he added to his drawings of textile machines. It was only in the sixteenth century that true lace was developed and from then until the nineteenth century lacemaking was widespread and well organised by people who knew what the market wanted. During the later part of this period, about which we know more, it was a sweated industry.

John Heathcoat of Nottingham, later of Tiverton, was the key figure in the early development of machine-made lace. Later, new methods of manufacturing machine lace were introduced and although adequate copies of hand-made work were produced the artistic qualities of hand-made lace have not been challenged.

Braids

There is another branch of fabric making which, although merging imperceptibly into sections already described, is better kept separate, namely the manufacture of narrow fabrics or braids. The most important group of these consists of very narrow loom weaving but such fabrics can be made without actual weaving, the yarns being twisted and intertwined with each other.

Primitive societies have frequently made these narrow fabrics, probably because they do not call for any complicated or large apparatus and so are suited to the nomadic life. In some cases, notably with certain African textiles, these fabrics have been sewn together to form cloths of any width required but more often braids have been used as decoration on other fabrics and as such comprise a wide and interesting part of textile design, though they have not achieved the artistic heights that other sections have.

Felts

Finally, there is a type of fabric which does not depend on

weaving, knitting or even on the manufacture of a yarn, namely felt. Historically, the process of felting has been confined to wool and is based upon the natural properties of the wool fibres to stick together when treated with heat to form a fabric. Felts tend to be rather thick and their application is limited. They do not lend themselves well to design effects and consequently the part they have played in the history of textile design is small.

The fabric is formed by pressing the hot wet fibres together, a technique which goes back to early times and has always had a greater vogue in the Middle East than elsewhere. Felts can be decorated by some form of printing once they are made or pieces of felt of different colours can be sewn on, a method sometimes known as intarsia. As most felts tend to lack suppleness they are unsuitable as apparel textiles.

The felting of wool produces a soft handling and warm fabric and this property was much sought after in the middle ages but in order to produce a more supple fabric it was common to make either a woven or, later, a knitted fabric first and then felt it, thereby producing a cloth which looked like a felt but, if analysed, will be found to be based on individual threads. Superfine broadcloth was made in this way.

4. Geographical distribution

Primitive

Primitive cloths are usually of more interest historically than artistically. By far the best collection of early fabrics consists of those that have been found in Egyptian tombs. They are usually of linen and represent a high degree of sophistication in the fineness of the spinning and weaving. The decoration is almost always by painting, which may be regarded as a form of printing. Complicated weaving is not sought. Elsewhere in other early sites almost all the fabrics found have been utilitarian. The preservation of textiles is largely a matter of chance, depending upon the right physical conditions, and Scandinavia has proved the best source. Most early Scandinavian fabrics are utilitarian and made in the plain or 2/2 twill. In other countries, although we have no physical remains, it is possible to get an idea of what cloths were like because sometimes the weave is imprinted on an accompanying piece of pottery.

Classical textiles tend to be uninteresting. Neither the Romans nor the Greeks, despite their great gifts in other directions, appear to have been brilliant textile designers. The Romans preferred plain colour effects and for their togas wanted a clear white background. As a result they paid much more attention than any previous race had done to breeding sheep that produced white wool. When they used colour they preferred the famous imperial purple, which was used as a symbol of rank. With the coming of the Byzantine civilisation, the position changed and textiles were produced which are amongst the finest in the world. Heraldic animals of great complexity were woven in designs and Byzantine fabrics have rarely been surpassed.

Coptic textiles are a special case. The Copts, who were a Christian sect living in Egypt, produced unique textiles of great beauty. Because the climatic and physical conditions of Egypt are ideal for the preservation of textiles we have an outstanding collection of Coptic works.

A different but important branch of primitive textiles consists of those fabrics made by so called primitive people today. There are many examples of these and the subject could be subdivided into peasant work and the more strictly primitive type still carried out by African weavers and also by such people as the Maoris in New Zealand. Particularly notable were the textiles of Peru but these will be described in the American section of this survey.

The study of peasant textiles is a vast subject. Such fabrics are of great ethnographical interest and often of considerable artistic appeal.

African textiles are limited in scope and most of the examples in museums today come from Nigeria, which has a remarkable tradition of weaving narrow fabrics on a rather specialised loom and sewing them together into attractive garments. This is quite a different approach to European and, to some extent, Asiatic peasant art, where a plain garment is usually decorated with embroidery. Primitive textiles from the Far East have been little studied. For a textile designer today the excellence of primitive design is impressive and presents a field of study where much is to be learnt.

Oriental

The history of Chinese textiles has been widely discussed and it has long been recognised that Chinese fabrics constitute one of the greatest of all textile traditions. Many of the best Chinese paintings are done on silk but these are not included here: the silk is merely a medium for the different art of painting. Although earlier fragments are known, the history of Chinese textiles begins with the great works of the Han dynasty, which have survived in remarkable numbers. From then until the nineteenth century China continued to produce beautiful works of art in the textile field. This great tradition continues and, indeed, is attracting increased interest today.

Indian textiles come into a different category and the main tradition is in the field of what are best called printed and painted calicoes. Cotton was the great fibre of the early Indian civilisations and many and varied techniques were evolved for producing on this fibre some of the most complicated patterns ever known. The impact in Europe of printed and painted calicoes from India has been emphasised. Later there was a more specialised type of Indian textile, the cashmere shawl, which was the germ of the shawl industry that was so important in Europe and America in the nineteenth century.

The great textile achievement of the Turkish and Persian world was the carpet, which represents a distinctive branch of textile art, certainly one of the greatest and also one that has in its mechanised form spread throughout the world. Persian carpets are more luxurious than Turkish but both belong to the same school.

European

The medieval centuries, from about AD 600 until 1500, were the greatest period of textile design in Europe and one of the greatest in world history. The medieval church was mainly responsible for this great flowering, which should be seen as part of the Romanesque and Gothic tradition. Most of the textiles produced were woven to make clear to the population the glories of the church. The tapestries of Angers were alternatives to paintings, serving the same purpose as the great frescoes of Italy. The other great masterpieces, the embroidered copes, were the garments worn by the high dignitaries of the same church. What percentage of these great textiles were devoted entirely to ecclesiastical use is not clear but they do appear to have been the majority. Nevertheless, these great textiles can only have been a small proportion of vast quantities that were made for everyday use. Some were completely utilitarian and not decorated; many were decorated in simple fashion. They are, perhaps, best illustrated by some of the examples of medieval printed linens which are found in many textile museums. For the everyday wear of the ordinary individual we largely have to depend upon chance finds.

The great broadening of civilisation during the Italian Renaissance led to an equal development in textiles. The magnificent Italian textiles of the period were often made in silk. They can be illustrated by many examples. It was generally considered that velvets were the most magnificent of all, usually deriving from Venice but also made elsewhere. The manufacture of velvets needed a high degree of technical skill. Some of the yarns, usually in the warp but sometimes in the weft, were cut after the cloth had been woven and in this way the pile stands upright. The effect was similar to that obtained by knotted carpets but these Italian velvets were often made from silk and this gave an unrivalled brilliance of colour and handle. A good way to appreciate the greatness of Italian textiles is to look at some of the paintings by the great artists of the time. Rarely, if ever, have people worn more magnificent clothes than did the Renaissance princes.

After 1500 European textiles continued the great traditions of previous years without maintaining quite the same high standard. Embroideries declined but the Flemish tapestry-weaving centres maintained the great traditions shown in the works at Angers. Later, other centres produced works that were fine but not as excellent as the earlier achievements.

In Spain basically similar traditions were followed but there were special elements, many of them derived from the Moorish influence in Spanish culture, which made the whole field of Spanish textiles distinctive.

British

Britain, in its Opus Anglicanum, English medieval embroidery, had one of the great early traditions of textiles but on the whole this was not maintained after the fifteenth century. Perhaps the importance of the British trade in fine woollen cloths, where handle and colour rather than the beauty of the design were the dominant features, led to this change. Later printed calicoes had their effect: from the design point of view, the coming of the factory and the mass-produced printed cloths of the nineteenth century added to the decline. The reaction began with such people as William Morris and has continued ever since. The revival of craft designing in the twentieth century has led, and continues to lead, to the production of fabrics which will, it is hoped, in the end rival the masterpieces of the past.

American

American textiles cover a wide and varied field and can conveniently be divided into three groups: first, those of the early American civilisations, of which the Peruvian textiles are outstanding; secondly, primitive American textiles, of which the fabrics of the Navajo Indians, now rather debased, are perhaps the best known and those of the Chilkat Indians are artistically the most interesting; thirdly, the fabrics made by the early white settlers in America, notably the coverlets.

These three groups – and others could be added – are quite separate and all that they have in common is that they were made in America. All have been well studied. The Peruvian textiles are very remarkable, being amongst the most varied we have from a primitive race. We are fortunate in having so many, because the climate of Peru has favoured their preservation. In their designs the Peruvians used many combinations, not only single and double cloth structures but also almost every possible form of warp and weft figuring. They combined normal weaving with tapestry weaving and added all kinds of extra decoration such as feathers. Few textile designers have been so ingenious. It is interesting to consider why these people were so successful with their textiles. Perhaps it was because they had, in the hair of the llama, one of the best fibres known in the world and even better, the hair of the vicuna, a fibre that today is the most expensive of all and was, at the time of the Aztecs, reserved for the special garments of the kings and priests.

Although much work has been done on the textiles of ancient Peru dating still remains uncertain. It would seem that the earliest come from a civilisation existing about 1000 BC; then, in the first millennium AD the Nazca culture produced perhaps the best of all. In the twelfth century came the rise of the Inca civilisation, and these people gradually conquered the rest of the area. Because the Incas were there when Pizzaro arrived, historians at first considered them the geniuses of the Peruvian civilisation but the study of the textiles and the pottery has made it clear that this was not the case. The brilliant work came earlier and it is only the accident of history that has given the Incas the fame that has come to them.

The modern textile designer can draw inspiration from examining these brilliant fabrics. One of the weaknesses of modern textile design has been its failure to give structural significance, and this the Peruvians were able to do. They used varying fibres, made yarns of varying size and combined them in fascinating ways, so giving exceptional depth to their work.

Modern

The reaction against the stereotyped designs arising from the techniques of the industrial revolution was led by William Morris and his followers and proved to be the beginning of a renaissance. There were other reasons, not least the increased knowledge and interest in primitive and peasant textiles from all parts of the world and a greatly increased knowledge of the early history of some of the great fabrics. Perhaps most important of all, and this derived especially from Morris, was the return to the textile scene of the hand craftsman. Many excellent fabrics are produced by machines but now, as in the past, the finest are hand-made with the individuality that can then be introduced.

As the twentieth century moves to its close there is evidence that this trend will continue, and as more and more people become more deeply involved then the knowledge of what has been produced in the past will become more valuable.

5. Museums

Anybody who becomes interested in textile history will obtain much pleasure by looking at great textiles. A few museums are devoted entirely to them; others may have just a few examples, sometimes almost hidden behind other works. Some of the best are listed below.

UNITED KINGDOM

The American Museum in Britain, Claverton Manor, near Bath, Avon. Telephone: Bath (0225) 60503. Housed in a most attractive manor house, this museum shows various aspects of American life and contains an impressive collection of American quilts and coverlets.

Bethnal Green Museum, Cambridge Heath Road, London E2. Telephone: 01-980 2415. A section of the Victoria and Albert Museum with a fine collection of Spitalfields silks.

Bowes Museum, Barnard Castle, County Durham. Telephone: Teesdale (0833) 37139. This famous treasure house, which contains wonderful paintings and furniture, also has good textiles, both tapestries and costumes.

Gallery of English Costume, Platt Hall, Platt Fields, Rusholme, Manchester. Telephone: 061-224 5217. With the Costume Gallery at the Victoria and Albert Museum, and the Museum of Costume at Bath, this is the leading collection in England.

Greater Manchester Museum of Science and Industry, Liverpool Road, Castlefield, Manchester M3 4JP. Telephone: 061-832 2244. A wealth of exhibits relating to the industry of the region is housed in the buildings of the world's oldest passenger railway station. Working displays of textile printing can be seen in the Warehouse Exhibition.

Hardwick Hall, near Chesterfield, Derbyshire. Telephone: Chesterfield (0246) 850430. This great country house has an unrivalled collection of tapestries, even without the famous Hunting pieces that have gone to London.

Kelmscott Manor, near Lechlade, Gloucestershire. This was William Morris's house, now owned by the Society of Antiquaries. It contains a good collection of Morris textiles.

Museum of Costume, Assembly Rooms, Alfred Street, Bath, Avon. Telephone: Bath (0225) 61111. Based originally on the private collection of Doris Langley Moore, this is one of the best museums of costume in England today. It is particularly valuable because, in addition to historical works, it is kept up to date with contemporary textiles.

Museum of Mankind (British Museum Department of Ethnography), 6 Burlington Gardens, London W1. Telephone: 01-437 2224. This museum contains one of the finest collections of primitive textiles in the world. Excellent exhibitions are mounted and large quantities are hidden away and not readily accessible. However, the special exhibitions are very important.

Museum of Scottish Tartans, Comrie, Perthshire. Telephone: Comrie (0764) 70779. This museum is devoted to tartans and presents a rich account of the development of this popular textile design.

Quarry Bank Mill, Styal, Cheshire SK9 4LA. Telephone: Wilmslow (0625) 527468. One of the great centres of the early industrial revolution. The buildings and machines have been restored to give an excellent reconstruction of an early mill.

Royal Albert Memorial Museum, Queen Street, Exeter, Devon. Telephone: Exeter (0392) 56724. Notable for its good collection of lace, particularly from Honiton. The museum publishes an excellent pamphlet on Honiton lace by Miss P. Inder.

Royal Museums of Scotland, Chambers Street, Edinburgh. Telephone: 031-225 7534. Covers many aspects of textiles, including an outstanding collection of documents on Turkey red dyeing.

Strangers' Hall Museum, Charing Cross, Norwich, Norfolk, Telephone: Norwich (0603) 611277, extension 275. Excellent material relating to the Norwich shawl industry: see the useful pamphlet *Norwich Shawls* by P. Clabburn. The interesting pattern books relating to the Norwich worsted industry are now at the Bridewell Museum in the same city.

Ulster Museum, Botanic Gardens, Belfast, Northern Ireland. Telephone: Belfast (0232) 668251. Probably the best museum in the United Kingdom for linen and with the finest collection of hand spinning wheels in the world. See the excellent pamphlet *Spinning Wheels*, published by the museum.

University Museum of Archaeology and Anthropology, Downing Street, Cambridge CB2 3DZ. Telephone: Cambridge (0223) 359714. A wonderfully rich collection of primitive and native textiles.

Victoria and Albert Museum, Cromwell Road, South Kensington, London SW7. Telephone: 01-589 6371. The museum has probably the finest textile collections in the world. Two groups should be specially mentioned: the tapestries, excellently shown in the new galleries, especially the Hunting tapestries, and the wonderful collection of English medieval embroidery.

Wallace Collection, Hertford House, Manchester Square, London W1. Telephone: 01-935 0687. Famous for its paintings and furniture but also contains many eighteenth-century textiles.

Welsh Folk Museum, St Fagans, near Cardiff. Telephone: Cardiff (0222) 569441. This folk museum, besides containing much interesting textile material, also has a complete small Welsh textile mill.

Whitworth Art Gallery, University of Manchester, Whitworth Park, Manchester M15 6ER. Telephone: 061-273 4865. This is, after the Victoria and Albert Museum, probably the most important collection of textiles in the United Kingdom.

EUROPE

Musée de Cluny, 6 Place Paul-Painlevé, Paris, France. Contains a wide variety of textiles but is best known for the Lady with the Unicorn tapestries, six panels of which are particularly well shown.

Musée de la Reine Mathilde, Bayeux, France. Contains the best known of all medieval embroideries.

Musée de L'Impression sur Etoffes, 3 rue des Bonnes Gens, Mulhouse, France. The chief museum in the western world for printed textiles.

Musée des Arts Décoratifs, Pavillon de Marsan, 107-109 rue de Rivoli, Paris, France. The museum owns what is perhaps the largest collection of textiles in the world, comparable with that at the Victoria and Albert Museum and the Metropolitan Museum of Art, New York.

Musée Historique des Tissues, 34 rue de la Charité, Lyons, France. One of the great textile museums of the world. As would be expected in Lyons, the silks are outstanding.

Museo Textil Biosca, Tarrasa, Spain. By far the most important textile museum in Spain and, although smaller, containing treasures that place it almost in the same class as the London, Paris and Lyons museums.

National Art Collections, Wawel 5, Krakow, Poland. Contains the tapestries woven for the King of Poland which are, with those at Angers and the Victoria and Albert Museum, probably the finest in the world. The Turkish tents are almost as remarkable.

Tapestry Museum, Chateau d'Angers, Angers, France. The Apocalypse Tapestries, arguably the greatest in the world, are now admirably shown in the special gallery built to house them.

There are many other great collections, particularly in America, where those at the **Metropolitan Museum of Art** in New York are perhaps the foremost. Another important collection is in Toronto, at the **Royal Ontario Museum**, which, in addition to its collection, has done much research and publication in the field.

The treasures of the **Hermitage** in Leningrad are legendary, and the finest museum of eastern printed textiles is the **Calico Museum of Textiles** at Ahmedabad in India. One cannot appreciate the greatness of Chinese textiles without visiting museums there and in Japan. Of a more specialised nature, Peruvian textiles are well represented in several museums but they cannot be fully enjoyed without seeing them in their country of origin.

Glossary

Abb: alternative name for weft.

Alencon: a point lace made in the French town of this name and capable of being constructed into forms of great beauty.

Alpaca: the hair of the alpaca, a type of llama found in South America; very soft handling. It was much used in Peruvian textiles and is very popular today.

Angora: the hair of the Angora rabbit, which has a very soft handle and is used for making soft fabrics for children's wear and in the past for dresses. It should be distinguished from the Angora goat, which produces mohair – a different fibre.

Axminster: originally a knotted pile carpet of British manufacture, woven on a hand loom in the Devon town that gave the name. Later a machine-made Axminster was developed.

Backed cloths: cloths which are made heavy by using an extra warp or weft. Can also be used for extra figuring, as explained in the text.

Baize: a heavy woollen cloth, well felted, and usually raised on both sides.

Bandanna: a handkerchief cotton or silk in which spots or figures are left white on a blue or red ground.

Bast fibres: fibres derived from the inner bark of plants or shrubs. Flax, hemp, jute and ramie are typical examples.

Bays: cloth made of worsted warp and woollen weft, first manufactured in England in the sixteenth century, especially in Essex and particularly at Bocking. Bocking bays were famous.

Beaver: a heavy milled woollen cloth with a raised finish, resulting in a nap like a beaver's skin.

Beer: a term denoting forty threads of warp, a convenient number for a warper to hold in his hand at one time. Sometimes spelt *bier*.

Beetling: the process by which some fabrics, particularly linen, are beaten, thereby flattening the fibres and producing a typical linen fabric.

Blackface: the most common sheep in Britain, producing coarse wool used for many purposes including the manufacture of Harris tweed.

Bleaching: the process of improving the whiteness of textile materials.

Block printing: the original method of printing with hand blocks, now largely replaced by roller and screen printing.

Bobbinet: a lace made by hand with bobbins and pillow; alternatively the machine-made equivalent.

Bobbin lace: made by intertwining threads on pins stuck on to a cushion. Also known as pillow lace.

Bombazine: a fabric, usually black, made of worsted warp and silk weft, originally a speciality of Norwich.

Botany: a generic term covering the best wool and the yarns and fabrics made from it. The word derives from Botany Bay, New South Wales, and emphasises the superfine nature of these wools.

Broadcloth: originally any cloth made on the broad loom, but later a fine cloth, woven in the plain weave, but heavily milled. Yorkshire broadcloths were sometimes called Leeds cloths after the place where they were chiefly made, but West of England broadcloths were the finest and the best.

Brocade: usually a silk cloth figured with metallic threads, which used to be commonly gold and silver. The term is sometimes used more widely to indicate a very fancy figured design.

Brussels: a heavy carpet usually with a looped rather than a cut pile.

Buckram: a strong linen cloth woven plain and stiffened. The word occurs quite often in Shakespeare's plays.

Buckskin: fine woollen cloth with a milled and dressed finish showing a distinctive twill.

Burling: the picking from the face of finished wool textiles of the remains of burrs and knots. Burrs come from the original vegetable matter in the wool and knots from repairs made in spinning and weaving.

Calico: white cotton cloth prepared for printing.

Calico printing: the most usual method of colouring cotton cloth in varied and attractive designs.

Callimancoes: a worsted cloth made originally in Norwich and then in West Yorkshire.

Cambric: a very fine plain woven linen, originally made at Cambrai in France. Also now applied to cotton cloths.

Cashmere: the wool of the Tibetan goat. Probably the finest and loveliest of all fibres. The word has occasionally been badly corrupted to denote torn-up knitwear.

Cheviot: the breed of sheep native to the Cheviot hills. A good dual purpose sheep, giving crisp wool, hence the name for the distinctive Cheviot suiting. The best Cheviot suitings are not often made from pure Cheviot wool but from a mixture of this wool with New Zealand Halfbred and English Southdown.

Chintz: a finely printed and frequently glazed cotton cloth in bright designs.

Chlorination: the treatment of wool with chlorine to remove the surface scales and so prevent shrinking.

Cochineal: the scarlet dye obtained from the dried bodies of insects which gives the brightest of all natural dyes, especially when used with a tin mordant.

61

Combing: the preparatory process for long wools. The short fibre, the noil, is removed and the product, the top, is spun into worsted yarn.

Cord: fabric woven in a weave which gives a cord effect, down or across the fabric. Obtained by extending the plain weave in warp or weft.

Corduroy: a stout cotton cloth woven with a pile face in cords, the pile usually being cut to form velvety ridges along the length of the fabric.

Cotton: originally the name applied in English to fabrics manufactured in the Manchester area that were made of wool. It was only in the eighteenth century, when true cotton arrived in England, that the word took its present meaning.

Count: the system used for measuring the size of yarn, usually the number of hanks of unit length that weigh 1 pound (0.45 kg). Most woollen districts have their own numbering system, but the worsted basis (the number of hanks of 560 yards – 512 metres – to weigh 1 pound) was and is fairly generally used and has led to the most common method of judging wool fineness. Thus a 60s wool is one that would spin to a yarn of such a fineness that 60 hanks of 560 yards would weigh 1 pound. The cotton trade used a system based upon the number of hanks of 840 yards (768 metres) that weighed 1 pound. These traditional numbering systems of yarn sizes are tending to be replaced by the new Tex system. It is also becoming more common to give wool measurements in terms of microns.

Crape: originally a fine silk gauze with high twisted warp, now usually made in other fabrics.

Crossbred: wool from sheep which have been produced by crossing one breed with another. For commercial reasons, particularly in order to get good lambing rates, most non-Merino sheep today are crossbreds.

Cyprus: a fine black linen lawn fabric.

Damask: a figured fabric made with one warp and one weft, usually using the warp and weft sateen weaves interchanging.

Design paper: paper ruled with vertical and horizontal lines suitable for showing weaves. Also called point paper.

Diamond: a lozenge-shaped design obtained by reversing the twill weave in warp and weft. Many fine early cloths (*c* AD 1000) were made in this weave.

Discharge: a method of printing whereby the fabric is dyed a solid colour and then printed with a substance that removes the dye, thus producing a pattern.

Distaff: the cleft stick that holds the prepared fibre on the hand spinning wheel.

Dobby: an arrangement for raising and lowering the harnesses on a loom, hence the dobby loom.

Doeskin: a fine woollen cloth made in a five-end weave and dress finish.

Donegal: characteristic Irish tweed, made in the plain weave with specially prepared fancy yarn.

Double cloth: two cloths woven together and stitched by interchanging one of the warp or weft with the other weft or warp. Alternatively they can be stitched with extra yarn.

Doubling: the twisting together of two yarns, very common in certain branches of the trade. In the wool textile trade, yarns for worsteds are usually doubled. In the knitting trade yarns of almost any type of fibre are used in their doubled form.

Dowlas: a coarse linen originally made in Brittany.

Drafting: the attenuations of slubbings, slivers or rollers in drawing and/or spinning. There are two types of drafting: roller drafting, where the fibres are pulled away from each other by passing between pairs of rollers running at different surface speeds; and spindle drafting, where the attenuation takes place between a pair of rollers and a spindle that is both revolving and moving away from the rollers, thus inserting twist during drafting.

Draw loom: the old form of loom for fancy weaving, where the weaver, through the draw boy, had control of each warp end.

Dressing: the process of raising and then cutting the nap, usually of woven cloth, thereby giving the traditional dress finish. Sometimes the word is used to describe the preparation of the warp for the loom.

Drop box: the type of shuttle box, invented by Robert Kay, which made changing shuttles simpler and ultimately automatic.

Drugget: a coarse woollen textile fabric felted and usually raised on one side.

Ell: the old standard length for measuring cloth. It varied in different countries: Scottish ell 37.2 inches, English 45 inches, Flemish 27 inches, French 54 inches.

End: an individual thread of yarn either in spinning or in weaving with special reference to the warp.

Extract: waste that has been obtained by carbonising wool-cotton rags, the lowest type of waste that can be reused.

Face cloth: a fabric where either warp or weft predominates on the surface, usually the warp.

Felt: a fabric made by matting or felting together the fibres, there being no separate warp or weft. Sometimes woven cloths that have been heavily felted are called woven felts, which is rather a misnomer.

Felting: the matting together of wool fibres, once highly valued, now often regarded as a nuisance.

Fibres, man-made: all fibres manufactured by man as distinct from those that occur naturally. There are two main groups:

the so called regenerated cellulose type, of which viscose rayon is the most common; and the true synthetics such as nylon, terylene, acrilan, courtelle and so on.

Flannel: a woollen or worsted cloth in a plain colour, usually, if a woollen, fairly well milled; often, but not necessarily, grey in colour.

Flax: the fibre of the plant *Linum usitatissimum* spun and woven into linen fibres.

Flying shuttle: John Kay's great eighteenth-century weaving invention of a new method of hitting the shuttle across the loom, which, although it did not necessarily involve power, made the power loom possible.

Frieze: a heavy woollen cloth.

Fuller's earth: a clay once very popular for cleaning cloth and so called from its use by fullers.

Fulling: the shrinking of woollen cloth as a deliberate process, very widely used in the past to produce broadcloths of various qualities and alternatively known as tucking or waulking.

Fustian: a cotton cloth, perhaps originally made from linen, and one of the most common products of the early English cotton trade.

Gabardine: closely woven twilled cloths, widely used for raincoats.

Gauze: a lightweight fabric in which the warp threads are twisted round each other, giving a light open texture.

Gig: the teasel-covered nap raising machine.

Grey cloth: pieces of cloth just off the loom, especially if intended for piece dyeing.

Hackling or heckling: the process by which the fibres of flax are disentangled and made ready for spinning.

Hank: a length of reeled yarn. Yarn for hand knitting is often sold in hanks, and the standard yarn measurement is usually so called.

Harris tweed: genuine Harris tweed must be one hundred per cent Scottish and must have been spun, dyed, woven and finished on the islands of the Outer Hebrides.

Heddles: the cords or wires that the warp threads pass through in the loom and therefore controlling mechanisms of the loom: also called *healds*.

Hemp: a type of fibre somewhat inferior to flax and obtained from a variety of plants.

Herringbone: the weave effect obtained by reversing the direction of the twill.

Hessian: a coarse canvas made of jute or hemp.

Holland: a fine bleached linen.

Honiton: a lace made in Devon around Honiton, consisting of sprigs made on a pillow.

Hopsack: a weave based on the plain weave but with every end and pick duplicated. Also known as the matt and the celtic.

Huckaback: a weave that gives a ribbed effect, most widely used for linen goods.

Indigo: the most famous of all dyes, originally a natural dye but now made synthetically. The synthesis of indigo by the great German dyestuff chemist Baeyer was one of the key events in the development of the synthetic dyestuff trade. It has been very popular recently for dyeing jeans.

Jacquard: loom used for weaving very fancy cloths. It replaced the old draw loom and was invented by the Frenchman Jacquard.

Jenny: Hargreaves's famous spinning invention. It was essentially a multiple spinning wheel using spindle, that is twist, drafting.

Jersey: any knitted piece goods, but originally presumably the knitted fabrics made on the island of Jersey.

Jute: the fibre of *Corchorus capsularis* and *Corchorus olitorius*, mainly grown in India and used to produce jute fabrics.

Kemp: coarse hairs found in some types of wool which will not dye.

Kendal: the famous green cloth of the Lake District, made from Herdwick wool.

Kersey: an important coarse woollen cloth originally made in the East Anglian village of Kersey; later the main product of the Yorkshire woollen trade, where it was sometimes known as northern dozens.

Knop yarn: fancy yarn, that is yarn with some distinguishing feature other than normal colour, fineness, etc. Strictly speaking, knop yarns are the type of yarn where a knop (that is a small lump of fibre or yarn) distinguishes the structure. Perhaps the best example of all is the Donegal tweed, where knops of material are added late in the carding process to give the well known spotted appearance.

Lace: a fabric made of a network of threads wrought into meshes.

Lambswool: wool shorn from sheep less than six or eight months old which can be very soft handling but is sometimes liable to coarse hair and even kemps.

Lease: now usually the division of the warp between odd and even threads, i.e. made at the time of the warping; hence such phrases as lease rods.

Leaves: alternative name for loom shafts.

Linen: cloth made from flax.

Lingoes: in the Jacquard loom with its many hundreds of inter-lacings harnesses extending the full width of the loom cannot be used. They are replaced by heald cords with a lingoe (a weight) attached to each end.

Linsey wolsey: coarse cloth traditionally made with a mixture of linen warp and woollen weft.

List: same as *selvidge*.

Llama: the Peruvian goat, which gives an interesting fibre, in someways similar to mohair.

London shrinking: the finishing process whereby the cloth is damped and then allowed to resume its relaxed state so as to avoid shrinking later, especially during the making-up processes.

Madder: a very important red natural dye. The synthetic form is alizarine.

Mechlin: a light Belgian lace made of threads twisted and plaited together.

Melange: a mixture, now especially applied to melange printing (vigoureux printing), whereby colour is printed along the yarn or slubbing.

Melton: heavy woollen cloth, until recently widely used for overcoats.

Mercerise: the process by which cotton yarns and cloths are made lustrous by the application of caustic soda, invented by John Mercer.

Merino: originally a breed of Spanish sheep but now spread throughout the world, giving the finer types of wools.

Mohair: the hair of the Angora goat, produced mainly in Turkey, South Africa and the United States of America.

Mordant: the chemical agent used for fixing dyestuffs.

Mule: woollen spinning machine. The word was first applied to Crompton's famous machine which combined roller and spindle drafting. The woollen mule, the main form of which remained in the industry until recently, used only spindle drafting.

Mungo: the material obtained from tearing felted woollen cloths, consequently shorter than shoddy. The name traditionally arose because the Yorkshire manufacturer attempting to use this very short material was told by his spinner that it would not go (i.e. would not spin) and he replied 'It mun go'.

Muslin: a class of goods, usually cotton, distinguished by their lightness and openness of texture.

Nail: an old yarn measure, usually 2¼ inches (58 mm) in length.

Nap: the fibrous surface of cloth which is raised or cut down. Hence the word napping.

Narrow width: cloth under 44 inches wide (1,118 mm), usually 27 to 30 inches (686 to 762 mm). Also the very narrow fabric or braid which is only a few inches wide.

Needle loom: a new machine used for making needle fabrics. A number of layers of fibres are taken and a needling machine pulls fibres from one layer through to another, thereby producing a kind of fabric. This is one of the modern techniques for producing non-woven cloths.

Nep: yarn or fabric which shows little spots of unopened fibre, a serious fault perhaps most frequently occurring with wool.

Nettles: can be spun and used to weave a fabric; fairly common in Scandinavia in the past. Like many vegetable products, nettles can be used to produce a yellow dye.

New Zealand flax: the plant *Phormium tenax*, which gives a fibre similar to low grade traditional flax.

Noil: the short fibre from the worsted combing process. An important material for the woollen trade.

Optical bleach: term sometimes used to describe a fluorescent brightening agent which improves the brightness of a fibre without performing a real bleaching operation. It compares with the traditional blue bag of the family household.

Organzine: silk thread produced by doubling together single reeled silk fibres.

Pattern chain: the chain that controls the interlacing of the warp and weft in weaving.

Pegging plan: the paper plan that indicates how the pattern change should be made.

Pick: the thread carried across the warp during one passage of the shuttle by the shuttle or other container.

Picker: the block of leather that hits the shuttle across the loom.

Piece: length of finished cloth, often about 70 yards (64 metres) but would have been shorter, say 25 yards (23 metres), in the days of hand weaving.

Piecer: the worker, usually a woman, employed in repairing the broken ends during spinning, particularly on the mule.

Pilling: accumulation of small clusters of entangled fibres on the surface of fabrics, especially liable to happen with certain synthetics.

Pillow lace: the kind of lace made by intertwining threads on pins stuck into a pillow over a pattern fastened underneath. Honiton, Mechlin, Irish, Buckingham and Valenciennes are all varieties of this type of lace.

Plain weave: the design or cloth pattern in which each thread of weft passes alternately over and under a thread of warp.

Plush: a cloth with a pile finish.

Ply: twist of a yarn where two or more threads are put together. The number is indicated by two-ply, three-ply, etc.

Point lace: lace made with a needle, as opposed to pillow lace.

Prunelle: name of the two and one twill or one and two twill.

Rack: alternative name for the tenter frame.

Raddle: rows of pegs used in beaming the warp in order to keep the threads straight and untangled.

Ramie: the fibre obtained from the inner bark of the plant *Boehmeria nivea*, sometimes known as China grass. Probably not as widely used as in the past.

Reed: the name given to the loom part which is removable and which consists of wires set between slats, used to control the set of the warp. An important part of the loom.

Rep or Repp: a corded fabric, usually weft wise, produced by weaving two, three or more picks of weft in one warp shed.

Resist printing: one of the methods of printing patterns on the cloth. A substance that resists the dye is printed on and, as this stays white in dyeing, the pattern is formed.

Ribbon loom: a weaving machine used for making very narrow fabrics.

Ringframe: the spinning machine on which the spindle revolves within a ring on which there is a small hoop, usually called a traveller. The most common form of machine spinning today.

Rock: an alternative name for the distaff.

Rope walk: the long walk in which ropes are laid on the hand ropemaking machine.

Sateen: a cotton imitation of satin, sometimes called Italian cloth.

Satin: a broken twill weave planned so that no two adjacent warp threads are crossed by weft in succession; a silk fabric woven broken twill with tram weft and organzine warp; a cloth woven broken twill with a worsted back or warp and a silk face or weft, or the reverse.

Saxony wool: a high grade of wool originally obtained from Saxony in Germany, also the fine yarn and particularly the cloth made from it. In fabric form it is always a woollen as opposed to a worsted fabric, probably because when these Saxony wools first came from Germany in the early years of the nineteenth century they were used entirely in the woollen trade.

Selvidge: sometimes selvage, another name for the list, i.e. the edge of a piece of cloth. Selvidges in certain modern types of loom are quite different in structure from the traditional selvidge, as each pick of weft is inserted as a separate entity.

Serge: originally a worsted warp, woollen weft cloth, widely made around Exeter. Now an all-worsted cloth, usually, but not necessarily, dark blue (navy). In the 1920s a navy botany serge was the most fashionable wear for men.

Shalloon: a worsted cloth used for making men's suits, widely manufactured in Yorkshire in the eighteenth century.

Shearing: has two meanings, firstly the clipping of the wool from the sheep, and secondly the levelling of the nap on the woven cloth. The latter process is sometimes called cropping or cutting.

Shed: the opening of the warp threads so that the weft can pass through.

Shepherd check: the four and four colouring on the two and two twill. The name originated in Scotland.

Shetland wool: particularly soft-handling wool from Shetland sheep. Unfortunately the word is now applied to a great many garments that do not have any Shetland wool in them.

Shoddy: the material obtained by pulling unmilled cloth. There has been a tendency recently to use the word to cover all types of pulled material.

Shoot: alternative name for weft.

Silk: the fine fibre spun by the caterpillars of moths belonging chiefly to the *Bombyx* genus. The silk fibre, which is in very long lengths, is reeled and then several strands of this reeled silk are twisted or thrown to produce silk yarn. However, much silk is damaged in reeling and some is not reeled at all. This silk is spun on traditional machinery and is usually known as spun silk.

Sisal: a kind of hemp derived from the *Agave sisalana* and widely used for twine and other purposes.

Slipe: the wool taken from a sheep that has been killed for its meat, but not the wool taken from a sheep that has died from natural causes.

Sprang: an early form of making a fabric which in appearance resembles knitting but in practice was made quite differently by interlacing the yarn between rods. Much used in Scandinavia. See the excellent book by P. Collingwood, *The Technique of Sprang*.

Stenter: alternative name for tenter.

Tammy: a cotton warp, worsted weft cloth in fancy colours, usually highly glazed.

Tappet: a cam which controls the harnesses and is used to describe the type of loom where the shedding is done by means of tappets.

Tartan: the checked pattern originating from the traditional Scottish tartan and now very widely made.

Teasel: the head of the thistle-like plant *Dipsacus fullonum*, in the past very widely used for raising the surface of woollen cloth.

Temple: the appliance which keeps the cloth stretched in the loom at the correct width.

Tenter: a machine used for drying cloth and also for removing any creases and straightening it before further processing. Originally this was done on tenter racks which were a common sight in all clothmaking areas.

Terry: a looped fabric where the pile is not cut, made by looping up the pile warp on the loom with the reed.

Thrum: the surplus ends of cloth, particularly of warp only, coming from the loom.

Tops: the slivers of fibre produced by the comb during worsted processing.

Tram: the silk yarn made by twisting singles and then used for weft. Less heavily twisted than organzine.

Tussah: wild silk. It is not reeled but spun in the traditional manner.

Tweed: originally a cloth made in the lowland area of Scotland, the term is now used for a wide variety of woollen cloths having effects produced by colour and design combinations. The word did not come from the river Tweed but from the misreading of the word twill.

Twills: one of the most popular of all weaves, the warp and weft combine to show a fine line running diagonally across the cloth.

Union: a fabric woven of mixed flax and cotton, wool and cotton or wool and jute. Historically it is of wool and cotton. The fibres may be mixed before or after spinning.

Vicuna: the undercoat, that is the fine part of the fleece, of the vicuna, a kind of llama. It produces a remarkably soft and fine fibre, today the most expensive in the world and originally reserved for the clothes of the Aztec princes.

Warp: the threads which run lengthwise in the cloth.

Weft: the threads that run across the cloth.

Woad: the ancient blue dye. The colouring principle is the same as indigo.

Woof: alternative name for weft.

Worsted: now used to define that type of fabric that is made from yarn spun on the worsted as opposed to the woollen principle, where the short wool has been removed and the yarn spun from tops. The name derives from a Norfolk village but worsted cloths made from combed wool were made long before the use of the name.

Bibliography

Antony, P. and Arnold, J. *Costume, a General Bibliography*. 1974.

Arnold, J. *A Handbook of Costume*. 1973.

Arts Council. *Opus Anglicanum. English Medieval Embroidery*. 1963.

Bell, Q. *On Human Finery*. 1976.

Brunelo, F. *The Art of Dyeing in the History of Mankind*. Vicenza, 1973.

Costume. Journal of the Costume Society. 1967-.

English, W. *The Textile Industry*. 1969.

Floud, P. *English Printed Textiles 1720-1836*. 1960.

Geijer, A. *The History of Textile Art*. 1979.

Gulvin, C. *The Tweedmakers: a History of the Scottish Fancy Woollen Industry 1600-1914*. 1973.

Houston, M.G. *A Technical History of Costume*. Second edition 1954.

Irwin, J. and Brett, K.B. *Origins of Chintz*. 1970.

James, J. *The History of the Worsted Manufacture*. 1957.

Jones, M.E. *British and American Tapestries*. 1952.

Jones, M.E. *The Romance of Lace*. 1951.

Lamb, V. *West African Weaving*. 1975.

Lawrie, L.G. *A Bibliography of Dyeing and Textile Printing*. 1949.

Montgomery, F.M. *Printed Textiles: English and American Cottons and Linens 1700-1850*. 1970.

Pond, G. *An Introduction to Lace*. 1968.

Ponting, K.G. *A History of the West of England Cloth Trade*. 1957.

Powys, M.L. *Lace and Lace Making*. 1953.

Reed, J. *Elementary Textile Designing and Textile Structure*. 1950.

Robinson, S. *A History of Dyed Textiles*. 1969.

Robinson, S. *A History of Printed Textiles*. 1969.

Stenton, Sir Frank. *The Bayeux Tapestry*. 1957.

Taussig, W. *Screen Printing*. 1947

Textile History, volumes 1-10.

Textile Institute. *Textile Terms and Definitions*. Seventh edition, 1975.

Thompson, F. *Harris Tweed*. 1969.

Thornton, P. *Baroque and Rococo Silks*. 1965.

Watson, W. *Textile Design in Colour. Elementary Weaves and Figured Fabrics*. Edited and revised Z. Grosicki. 1975.

Watson, W. *Advanced Textile Designing*. Edited and revised Z. Grosicki. 1977.

Wright, R.H. *Modern Designs and Production*. 1949.

Index